VATICAN, U.S.A.

Also by Nino Lo Bello

THE VATICAN EMPIRE

VATICAN, U.S.A.

by

Nino Lo Bello

TRIDENT PRESS
NEW YORK

Excerpt from The Rich and The Super-Rich *by Ferdinand Lundberg is published by arrangement with Lyle Stuart, copyright © 1968 by Ferdinand Lundberg. Excerpts from* The Case Against Congress *by Drew Pearson and Jack Anderson are reprinted with permission of Simon & Schuster, Inc., copyright © 1968 by Drew Pearson and Jack Anderson.*

TO IRENE ROONEY LO BELLO:

In deep appreciation of her open mind,
unshakable friendship and loving encouragement,
I dedicate this work with utmost affection.

CONTENTS

INTRODUCTION
THE FIRST TEN COMMANDMENTS
ARE THE HARDEST

In extracting the pure principles which Jesus taught, we should have to strip off the artificial vestments in which they have been muffled by priests, who have travestied them into various forms, as instruments of riches and power to themselves.—THOMAS JEFFERSON

"YOU BETTER read this carefully! It may be the last one you read! Somebody is going to put a bullet through your fat ass, you scum, you masculine lesbian bitch! I pitty you in your ignorince!"

"You will be killed before too long. Or maybe your pretty little baby boy. The queer looking basterd. You are a bitch and your son is a basterd."

Poison-pen letters like these are delivered almost every day to a modest little white house on Sinclair Road in a quiet suburban section of Austin, Texas. The house, when not being used as a home, serves as the headquarters and office of Mrs. Madalyn Murray O'Hair. The most famous atheist in America, Mrs. O'Hair achieved national publicity, while living in Baltimore, when her lawsuit got the United States Supreme Court to remove religious prayers from the public schools.

Ever since that time Mrs. O'Hair has had to endure an unbelievable array of insults, threats and obscenities, most of which reach her through the daily mail. Once she received an envelope containing a newspaper photograph of herself that was smeared with excrement. All such missives are filed by Mrs. O'Hair in a folder labeled "Letters from Christians," and she plans one day to publish these in a book bearing the same title.

Madalyn Murray O'Hair, far from being intimidated by the vitriolic correspondence, continues to fight against organized religion. Just as she fought her school-prayer case up to the Supreme Court in 1963, so does she expect to bring another suit to the high court—this suit having to do with churches and taxes. Speaking as a homeowner and a taxpayer, Mrs. O'Hair is of the view that her taxes, as well as everybody else's taxes, are inordinately high because church property is not proportionately taxed. In Baltimore Circuit Court she has filed suit for the levying of taxes on churches too. Although her suit names the tax officials of Baltimore as defendants, the Roman Catholic Archdiocese of Baltimore was granted the right to appear in the action in opposition, ostensibly because it stands to lose several million dollars if Mrs. O'Hair is successful in the courts.

"We are going to subpoena the Archbishop of Baltimore," Mrs. O'Hair explained, "and make him tell how much money the Church collects from its property in Baltimore, how much of that remains in Baltimore, how much remains in the United States, and how much goes to Rome. That information has never been available before. People can add and subtract, you know. Wait till the American public starts figuring out how low its taxes would be if all that untaxed money were not flowing out of the country."

In the preparation of this book, I spent a Saturday and half of a Sunday in the company of Madalyn Murray O'Hair and her husband, Richard. We met in their Texas office, the headquarters of the recently formed Poor Richard's Universal Life Church. Even though, in view of her militant atheism, Mrs. O'Hair's new "church" may exist in a kind of twilight haze, the organization is legally a tax-exempt church—exempt from federal taxation on income derived from interest, dividends, royalties or capital gains. As such, the "Reverend" Mrs. O'Hair maintains, it may now purchase and own, as well as operate, hotels, stores, mines, newspapers, farms, radio stations, office buildings, racetracks, cattle ranches, distilleries, drugstores, supermarkets and industries of every description. Moreover, she insists, Poor Richard's Universal Life Church will not need to pay taxes or file any financial reports, no matter how great the profits. Sitting in her kitchen-office and peering from behind piles of books, she explained the situation, citing each of the various sections of the Internal Revenue Code which give her new church full protection under the law.

Mrs. O'Hair was one of hundreds of people I visited and interviewed in connection with this book. The research took me to each of the fifty states of the union and to nearly two hundred major American cities. During my six-month auto swing across the face of America, I conferred with people in all walks of life. I was interested in speaking with anyone who had any professional interest in the subject of religion and, more especially, in the subject of Roman Catholicism. My investigation took me into the private chambers of many individuals who were not eager to respond to prying questions about Roman Catholic finances. Even ex-priests, who might have been expected to have an ax to grind with their former superiors, were frequently reluctant to discuss the Church's money affairs. But for every person who shied away from my inquiries there were dozens of others who were eager to help in whatever small way they could. This included, surprisingly, people who held positions of authority within the structure of the American Catholic Church—clergymen and laymen who were frank and honest and willing to let the chips fall where they might. And to my gratification as a newspaperman, I was pleased to discover how well informed editors in every state of the union were about religion and business in their respective areas.

Until I made this trip through America, I had not really known my country well. This was largely because work as a business-news foreign correspondent had kept me on the Continent for more than a dozen years. And actually it was on the Continent that this book had its origins, for it was an outgrowth of an earlier book, *The Vatican Empire*, published in 1969. That first book, an objective report which attempted to lift the cloak of secrecy surrounding the Vatican's extensive business operations, revealed how the Church has become one of the greatest fiscal powers in the world. The book was read and discussed behind Vatican walls and had more of an impact than one could have dreamed of. The reactions from the reading public in North America and Europe were impressive. Letters, ranging from pure praise to requests for more information to outright threats, came in like a flood.

The questions that were asked most frequently over and over again by the letter writers and newspaper interviewers were about the finances of the Roman Catholic Church in the United States. Unfortunately I could not shed much light on this subject, because my research had been undertaken in Rome and devoted exclusively to the Vatican. I knew little or nothing about the business activities of the Church in America. When it became obvious that a book needed to be written about Catholic money in the U.S., there was no other way to get the information than by penetrating the Catholic scene in each of the fifty states.

It is not the purpose of this book to pass judgment on the American Catholic Church, nor to examine the major conflicts that beset the religion today. Neither is it the purpose of this sequel to evaluate the relative merits of the tenets of the Catholic religion. This is a business book, and the purpose here is to examine the Church and its money. In pursuit of this elusive information, I took a leave of absence from my post in Europe and sailed for the beckoning shores of my native land.

During my travels, I consulted a great many persons. Unfortunately, they are too numerous to mention all of them by name but the omission does not imply any lack of appreciation, for I am as much indebted to them as I am to the following individuals.

For helping to flesh out sections of my inquiry and to work out the puzzle of American Catholic finances, I wish to express special thanks and appreciation to Martin Larson, Ph.D., and to C. Stanley Lowell, associate director of Americans United, a nonprofit corporation in Washington, D.C., dedicated to preserving the constitutional principle of church–state separation. Their book *Praise the Lord for Tax Exemption** was a marvelous source of information. Both Dr. Larson and Mr. Lowell placed their valuable time and knowledge at my disposal and gave encouragement and interest when this book was still only an idea.

Special thanks also go to "Bishop Tizio X," who read the various drafts several times and applied his extensive background and wisdom. Others who gave of their time and help were George M. Collins, Hugh McCann, Madalyn Murray O'Hair, Paul Blanshard, Lester Kinsolving, Jack Anderson, the late Drew Pearson, Ferdinand Lundberg, Lyle Stuart, Glenn L. Archer, Adele A. Porter, Elaine Bowers, Gioele Settembrini, Gaston D. Cogdell, Paul Gitlin, Eugene Winick, Barbara J. Hendra, Charles W. De Mangin, Carl E. Clemens, Jack Handley, Donald W. Gormley, Andrea Palmer, Thomas M. Reay, Donald L. Breed, Charla Jenkins, Selwyn Pepper, Hollis J. Limprecht, Kenneth Cole, Robert B. Smith, Harold

---

*Published by Robert B. Luce, Inc., Washington and New York, 1969.

Schellkopf, Richard Gill, Herbert Knowlton, Joseph J. O'Conor, Bernard Judy, Eugene Gauger, Lee Steele, Murlin B. Spencer, Jimmy Bedford, James L. Bracken, James B. King, Tom Swint, Beverly Russell, Louis R. Guzzo, Edwin J. Erlandson, Bert Gaskill, William K. Hosokawa, James Idema, Harold Schindler, Robert Blair, Lyle Olson, R. R. "Red" Kelso, Alton F. Baker, Jr., George Chaplin, Buck Buchwach, Adam A. Smyser, Carl Wright, Cornelius D. Downes, Shurei Hirozawa, Eugene Hill, Charles Irish, John Burns, Wilbur Kent, Dean Huber, Alan Pritchard, Douglas Hope, John Hurst, Gordon Pates, William German, Sid Allen, Stanleigh Arnold, Robert Gibson, Ernest Conine, John Hirt, Hank Greenspun, Vincent Anselmo, Richard Calhoun, John E. Leard, Charles E. Mahon, Clarke Bustard, John Fay, William M. Phillips, Scott Marshall, John S. Walters, Arthur B. Manning, Walter G. Cowan, Maury A. Midlo, Jay A. Gross, Wallace Carroll, Virtie Stroup, Weldon Wallace, Steve O'Neill, Earl Pruce, Wade H. Mosby, John Frankland, Robert W. Bliss, Robert E. Rhodes, Willmar Thorkelson, Herb Bechtold, Virgil Larson, Ross Phipps, Barney Laschever, James Mason, Ivan N. Robinson, James Devaney, George Gill, James S. Pope, Jr., Dickson Scott, Elmer von Feldt, Carl McIntire, Gordon Hanna, Emmett Maum, Gail Driskill, Jack L. Butler, Jack Douglas, Tom Simmons, Bob Wright, James Clark, George Carmack, Robert A. Brown, G. Ward Fenley, Mary Rose Badgley, J. Edward Murray, Tom Sanford, Ella Mae Mahon, Charlotte Burrows, Jack Gould, Cleo Gould, Charles H. Lindsay, Tyler Resch, Edward Kelly, Dick Burke, Chester Apy, Jack Kogan, Harry Rosenfeld, Ben Bagdikian, George H. Arris, Byron Israelson, Mary Sparrow, George Woodbury, Jim Berry, Kathy Haeberle, David I. Rimmel, Nanci Alden, Jack Sitton, Stephen Allen, Kathleen Rowley, Herbert H. Skirvin, Danuta S. Borowski, Andrew Wallace, Harold Gadd, Jay Clarke, George Christian, Donald A. Streater, Albin Gorisek, Jim Miller, Mark Dahlinger, Bruce Fishwild, Phyllis Fleming, Tom Kiene, Betty Medsger, Edward Quill, Robert G. Hoyt, James F. Andrews, Robert G. Olmstead, Arthur N. Winter, Betty Fitzpatrick, Donald J. Thorman, Frank Angelo, Dave Smith, Luis Bueno, Daniel Lupton, Milton Berkowitz, Charles T. Davis, Bill Lewis, Martha Douglas, Patricia Allen Roy, Leo Pfeffer, Albert L. Kraus, Murray M. Weiss, Paul Townsend, Vicki Renner, Vincent J. Lovett, George Malzone, Robin Lloyd, Stephen Wells, Avro Manhattan, Richard Godfrey, Terence Shea, Edward B. Fiske, Harry Graham, D. B. Robertson, James K. Beazley, Wilton Wynn, Paul Hofmann, Alfred Friendly, Jr., Robert Johnson, George W. Cornell, Bennett Bolton, Alfred Balk, Edward J. O'Donnell, Murray B. Light, Louis J. Putz, F. D. Cohalan, Edward A. Ryan, Henry J. Browne, Leonard L. Peterson, Richard F. O'Hair, Emmett Kelley, Thomas J. Gumbleton, Margaret Biron, Horace Contini, Oliver Dippold, George M. Downs, Ralph Ginzburg, Borden V. Mahoney, Corrado Pallenberg, Sonja Hansen Jacykewycz, Emilie Rooney, Robert Strauss, Anthony Calice, Anny Paulick, Bela von Block, Richard N. Ottaway, Augusta Winkler, Frieda Tighe, William A. Caldwell, Joseph O'Donoghue, Mario Tedeschi, Rudolph Bold and David Garrity.

And finally to my wife, Irene, a special note of appreciation for being the midwife who helped me give birth to this manuscript.

Most of the people I consulted did not know and do not know my religious preference, but as I am dedicated to unearthing the hard truth, this would be entirely irrelevant. I am a reporter. What I do Sunday mornings has no bearing on my work and has had, therefore, no bearing on this book.

In spite of the fact that millions of Catholics throughout the United States are simple, pious people who want only to worship their own God in their own way or do praiseworthy social work for others, critics of the Church like to assert that the authority within the Catholic Church is controlled by men who are chiefly power politicians masquerading under the cloak of religion. Whether or not this is a fair metaphor is not material for these pages. The topic here is not the merits or shortcomings of Catholicism; it is money. My task is to deal with the relationship between the American Catholic Church and its money, its riches, its wealth, its properties and its holdings. I offer no value judgments.

Experience suggests that no subject causes as many misunderstandings as does religion. It is not easy for a reporter to put down a set of facts about the Catholic Church without expecting controversy, especially if the subject relates to money—for it seems to be an unwritten commandment of the Catholic hierarchy that thou shalt not mention finances. Perhaps it is about time that people come to realize that in keeping the Church's physical and fiscal balance, the first Ten Commandments are indeed the hardest.

N. L. B.

Vienna, June 1972

16

1

HOUSE THAT WHO BUILT?

When the chips are down, money counts more than religion.
—JOHN F. KENNEDY

THE NATION'S CAPITAL is a place where the name of the game is name-dropping. Thus it is not difficult to understand why the $70-million Watergate cooperative apartment complex overlooking the Potomac River is the "in" place to live, for it is a politically star-studded attraction whose many Republican big-shot residents have helped it earn the nickname "the White House West."

Top government officials, many of them associated directly with President Richard M. Nixon's Cabinet or his staff, have found a togetherness at this capital castle, as have a number of G.O.P. Congressmen who have moved in. Providing a roof for half of the Presidential Cabinet, two of his secretaries, a speechwriter and editor and the chief of protocol, Watergate has many nice attractions, not the least of which is the fact that it is located "eight to ten minutes to or from the White House in traffic." Built on ten acres of Foggy Bottom rubble, Watergate has everything the Nixon people could desire. Within its plush walls are Washington's best pastry shop, a post office, a branch of the Riggs National Bank, a Safeway market, a People's Drug Store, a wine and liquor shop, outdoor café, restaurant, gift shop, barbershop, hairdresser, stationery store, health club and sauna, swimming pool, and a solarium. There are also an underground garage, closed TV circuits, an intercom system (which can also beam emergency messages to anyone riding up or down an elevator), a regular newspaper (*The Watergate Post*) and an extremely tight security setup.

Comprising two apartment buildings, a hotel, an office building and an additional wing that is half office and half residential, Watergate has become, since it was built a few years ago, a luxury landmark. Watergate East has a total of 240 posh apartments, while Watergate West has 143 dwelling units, most of which are sold or rented on a co-op basis. Apartments in Watergate sell for as high as $140,000 (the price that the then Attorney General John N. Mitchell and Transportation Secretary John A. Volpe paid for theirs), but the median price is about $65,000 for a two-bedroom dwelling. The cost of a Watergate apartment is determined by whether the living-room window faces the Potomac or whether it overlooks the Howard Johnson Motel across the street. A buyer usually puts up 43 percent of the purchase price, and mortgage payments plus maintenance and other services run to about $1,700 per month. Reservations for garage parking for residents come to $3,500 per automobile, with a down payment of $1,700; the $1,800 balance is paid in monthly installments. For those who prefer not to buy, the average rent for a three-room apartment can be as high as $1,400 a month, which is what Miss Rose Mary Woods, Mr. Nixon's private secretary, pays for a furnished duplex.

Most of the money to build Watergate came from the Vatican—by way of the world's largest construction company, the Società Generale Immobiliare of Rome. Since S.G.I. was the principal financier of the Watergate project, the Catholic

18

Church today is still a major holder of Watergate's stock. The two firms that sell, rent and administer for Watergate are accountable to the Vatican. Virtually from the beginning, Giuseppe Cecchi, who is vice-president of Watergate Improvements, has been on the scene to keep a Roman eye on things.

The neighboring Potomac Plaza Terrace co-op apartments are also part of Watergate Improvements, which developed it for the Vatican through SOGENE, a front company owned by S.G.I. As the oldest of Italy's construction companies (formed in September 1862 in Turin when that city was the capital of the young Italian nation), S.G.I. covers every facet of the building business—from planning to investment, from development to management, and from construction to the production of specialized building materials and equipment. After the Second World War S.G.I. branched out on a national scale, and in recent years, boasting assets of $200 million, it has moved into the international scene through associate or cousin companies, as in the case of the Watergate project, a "relative" two or three times removed. Except for some of the mother-company employees and stockholders, few people really know which of the related companies belong to S.G.I. and which are indirectly controlled by parental purse strings. Altogether, S.G.I. fronts for over fifty subsidiaries and, like a mother hen, prefers to shield them from too much direct light.

One of these subsidiary companies was Ediltecno, S.p.A., which when liquidated in 1967 was fully owned by S.G.I. Organized in 1961 to service projects abroad, Ediltecno was a technical, consulting and engineering management company which had branch offices in Washington and Paris and a representative in New York City. In Montreal there is a Canadian company known as Ediltecno (Canada) Limited and in Mexico City an affiliate called Ediltecno de Mexico, which serves as a parent company to the Lomas Verdes S.A. de C.V. construction company. On some 1,300 acres of scenic land outside Mexico City, near Tlalnepantla, Lomas Verdes built a suburban city which houses about 100,000 persons, and it also constructed a four-lane superhighway connecting the new city to the main road that leads to the center of the Mexican capital. Another Vatican-affiliated company, Inmobiliaria Corinto S.A., put up five sixteen-story apartment houses in Mexico City's fashionable Paseo de las Palmas neighborhood.

S.G.I. has also been active in Canada through its subsidiary companies. The Italian organization was the largest single stockholder in Montreal's Redbrooke Estate Ltd., with 85 percent of the shares. Redbrooke completed a thirty-three-story apartment building with three underground levels in the heart of one of the most fashionable sections of Montreal. It includes 224 apartment units and 100,000 square feet of indoor parking. Known as Port-Royal, the building is owned by a Vatican company called Immobiliare-Canada Limited, which has share obligations of $14.4 million, of which S.G.I. holds 93 percent. The same company took over a forty-seven-story office building built by the Place Victoria–St. Jacques Company, Inc. Called the Stock Exchange Tower because it houses the Canadian and Montreal Stock Exchanges, the building cost nearly $50 million in Canadian dollars and is believed to be the tallest reinforced-concrete building in the world. Another Vatican-controlled company in Canada is the Sogesan Construction Company Limited, which put up over 300 one-family houses southwest of metropolitan Montreal.

Following publication of *The Vatican Empire*, which disclosed for the first time that S.G.I. was largely controlled by the Roman Catholic Church, the Vatican announced it would sell up to 95 percent of its interest in the company. And during the middle part of 1969 the Vatican in an unprecedented press conference revealed it had negotiated the sale of its holdings in Società Generale Immobiliare to American interests. This was not quite the whole story, however. Later it became known that the buyer was Charles B. Bluhdorn, board chairman of Gulf & Western Industries, which owns the Paramount Pictures Corporation. Although the exact amount of Gulf & Western's shareholding in S.G.I. was not revealed, it became known that effective control of the company had been accomplished. The key man behind the deal was Michele Sindona, one of Italy's leading financiers and a lawyer who handles many American interests in Italy on behalf of the Bank of America, the Celanese Corporation and other firms. Mr. Sindona is one of the few men in the world to enjoy the confidence of both the Vatican and international American business companies.

To wrap up this deal, Mr. Sindona bought the 3.5 percent of S.G.I.'s shares owned by the Assicurazioni Generali, an Italian insurance company in which the Vatican has a heavy participation. Shortly afterward he was elected to S.G.I.'s board of directors. That Mr. Sindona should have negotiated the deal through the Paribas Transcompany of Luxembourg and on behalf of G. & W. came as no surprise. His Liechtenstein holding company, Fasco, and the Paribas bank together purchased a 40 percent stake in Libby & Company and sold it in 1966 to Nestlé for about $40 million. Mr. Sindona also sold his 26 percent holding in the Brown Company, a $250-million paper company which owns more than 600,000 acres of timberland in New England, to G. & W. in exchange for $16 million of G. & W. convertible debentures. The crucial role Mr. Sindona played in the S.G.I. deal is, therefore, a logical consolidation of existing holdings with both G. & W. and the Paribas bank.

Gulf & Western Industries, incorporated in Michigan in

1934 and reincorporated in Delaware in 1967, has its main offices in New York City. Doing an annual business of better than $1.5 billion, G. & W. is a conglomerate with operations in manufacturing, foods and consumer products, movies, film distribution, pulp and paper products and distribution. The products of its manufacturing division, which comprise about 42 percent of its business, include die castings, stampings and plating, forgings, aerospace parts, life-support equipment, electrical components, machinery and parts, ammunition and ordnance items. Its food and consumer products consist of sugar, fruit and vegetable production and the production of such name cigar brands as Dutch Master, El Producto and Muriel. G. & W. also has mines and is an integrated producer of zinc products, titanium dioxide pigments, metal powders, anhydrous ammonia and liquid carbon. Because of its recent dealings with Mr. Sindona and the Vatican, there had been some speculation as to what kind of financial interest Mr. Sindona or the Vatican might have had in G. & W., but there has been no evidence forthcoming from knowledgeable business sources, nor has the Vatican offered any clarifications other than the original S.G.I. sales announcement.

Though the Vatican sold most of its shares in S.G.I., it still retains a 5 percent interest, and its association with G. & W., whatever it may be, could signal higher corporate profits across the board. In any event, papal affiliation with S.G.I. was such that the Watergate apartment complex stands as a monument to the bigness of Vatican business. Watergate fires the imagination of people who are good at figures, and though it has nothing to do with the American Catholic Church, it contributes to the latter's super-rich image. Without fear of contradiction, one can deduce that the American Catholic Church is far and away the richest of all the American religions. A judicious estimate, based on this writer's accumulated information and observation, would put the combined total assets of all the Catholic units in the United States and Canada at better than $80 billion—with the cumulative annual income reaching nearly $12.5 billion.

Concurring with this calculation is Father Richard Ginder, a priest who writes a nationally syndicated column for Catholic publications. He says: "The Catholic Church must be the biggest corporation in the United States. We have a branch office in every neighborhood. Our assets and real estate holdings must exceed those of Standard Oil, A. T. & T. and U.S. Steel combined. And our roster of dues-paying members must be second only to the tax rolls of the United States Government."

2

SOUR SMELL OF SUCCESS

The American continents . . . are henceforth not to be considered as subjects for future colonization by any European powers.—JAMES MONROE

IN 1852 a group of eight nuns traveled by horseback from St. Louis to Santa Fe, New Mexico, where they settled down and began building a chapel. It was not completed until 1875. At the time, a staircase to the choir loft had to be omitted because it would have taken up more than half the floor space in the tiny chapel. To gain access to the choir loft, these Sisters of Loretto had to use a vertical ladder which was cumbersome, unsafe and a bit undignified. While they were seeking a solution to the problem, a "little old man" presented himself and asked permission to deal with the task.

According to historical records, the man set about his chore, but, curiously, no one saw him working on the staircase. When at length it was completed, it caused wonder. For it was a spiral stair with a vertical centerpost and was constructed without nails. The Sisters of Loretto wanted to pay the carpenter for his services but were unable to locate him. They went to every lumberyard and hardware store in the Santa Fe area to try to discover his identity, but the storekeepers reported that they had not sold materials needed for a staircase during the time of the construction. Meanwhile engineers and other experts who visited the chapel and marveled at the fine work could not explain its construction. In time, religious people began to wonder about that "carpenter" who had built the unusual wooden structure without nails. Was he not perhaps the Carpenter from Galilee?

The odd spiral steps, which soon became known as the Miraculous Staircase, were featured in Ripley's "Believe It or Not" and are visited by some ten thousand tourists each year. The world-famous names in the guest register of the little chapel include those of John F. Kennedy, Robert F. Kennedy, Hubert H. Humphrey, Prince Rainier of Monaco and Mrs. Eleanor Roosevelt.*

Santa Fe's Miraculous Staircase is a colorful footnote in the history of the Catholic people in the United States. American Catholicism, born of the most humble means, has not always met with favor. While early days in America were characterized by the law of the quick trigger, the rise of the Catholic Church was characterized, in large measure, by the law of the quick temper, which in turn created prejudices that still exist today in many places. Tracing the historical development of the American Catholic Church in complete detail from the early days of the Spanish and French Catholic missionaries who tried to Christianize the Indians in the sixteenth and seventeenth centuries is not within the scope of this book. A brief rundown suffices, if only to provide a background for under-

---

* In 1970 the Sisters of Loretto sold to the owners of a hotel across the street five acres of land which included the tiny chapel and the Miraculous Staircase. The sum of money involved was $700,000. But the terms of the sale stipulated that the staircase and the chapel could not be moved or destroyed for a minimum of a hundred years. While the acquired parcel of land would be used as a parking lot for hotel guests, the operators of the hotel will continue to maintain the chapel and staircase as a tourist attraction.

standing the growth of American Catholic wealth and power.

The point of origin of the American Catholic Church necessarily must be considered Baltimore. The Baltimore story began in 1634 when the second Baron Baltimore, Cecil Calvert, a Roman Catholic, became proprietor of a colony at St. Clement's Island in Chesapeake Bay. As the new settlers came, Lord Baltimore got the Church to send over a number of Jesuit priests with the understanding that they were not to expect any material financial aid from him or from the Catholic colonists. In accordance with this condition, two priests and a Catholic layman arrived and, while providing for their own needs, laid in substance the groundwork for the Catholic Church's future in the world of American business. Like every other colonist, they received a stipulated amount of land, and by working their land, in addition to carrying out clerical duties, they supported themselves.

A wooden house deserted by the local Indian tribe was converted into Maryland's first chapel, thereby becoming the first piece of church property in the colony. In 1637 Reverend Thomas Copley came to the colony and took general control of the mission. Father Copley was awarded his parcel of land, and for every five men he brought over, according to the law prevailing at the time, he was awarded two thousand acres. Altogether, Copley was responsible for bringing in nearly fifty men over a period of two years, so that the Jesuits did indeed accumulate extensive acreage. In addition Chief Maquaconen of the Patuxent tribe made a gift to Copley of a fertile tract of land, and a number of bequests from Catholic faithful were also adding to Copley's properties. The Jesuits were "in business." When there were signs of growing colonial displeasure with the Jesuits, and attempts were made to separate the Church from its holdings, the priests found ways and means to conceal their ownership and hold on to their multiplying possessions.

The practice of toleration established by the Baltimore family brought a number of religious sects into Maryland; since most of these were Protestant, it did not appear likely that the colony in Maryland would later become a Catholic stronghold.

In 1789 Pope Pius VI erected at Baltimore the first See in the United States. At the time, out of a total population of nearly four million there were only thirty thousand Catholics in the country, most of them in Maryland and Pennsylvania. Inspired by the Pope's recognition of the small American Catholic community, the Jesuits sought in a systematic way to add significantly to their property.

The only place in colonial America outside Maryland where Catholics were found in any number and with full legal toleration was Philadelphia, the capital of the colony founded by the Quaker William Penn. Later, in the 1790s, fugitive priests fleeing the revolution in France came to the New World in droves, and many of them went to the frontier of the trans-Allegheny West to link up the remnants of old French missions with Baltimore. Two sisterhoods were founded in 1818 to deal with this western Catholic expansion, while in the East the Sisters of Charity founded by Elizabeth Seton became the main women's society and remained such for nearly a quarter of a century. In 1822 Bishop John England founded the first American Catholic newspaper, *The United States Catholic Miscellany*. On the issue of church property there were some dissenting voices, but most of the states made statutory provisions for tax immunities.

It was the flood of Irish and German immigrants during the middle part of the nineteenth century, however, that gave the American Catholic population its first big boost—to nearly five million. The famine in Ireland and the political upheavals in Central Europe encouraged a flood of Catholic communicants to New World shores; 2.5 million came from Germany and 1.7 million from Ireland between 1841 and 1860. Others arrived from Austria, France, Italy, Poland, Russia and south-eastern Europe. After 1845, the face of American society underwent a drastic alteration.

A movement against this immigration engendered an anti-Catholic feeling that provided the background for many debates in the 1860s and the 1870s on the material status of the Church and the question of tax exemption. Intense concern over the matter was generated by President Ulysses S. Grant's expressed fear of "corporate accumulations, religious or otherwise." Later it was shown that President Grant's high estimate of church property had been incorrect. In 1894 Reverend Madison C. Peters threw some light on the subject when he reported that the value of the property owned by all religions in America had reached about $2 billion, with the holdings of the Roman Catholic Church coming to approximately $250 million.

Big Catholic population gains were made between 1881 and 1890, when 1,250,000 Catholic immigrants reached American shores. In 1890 there were nearly 9 million Catholics in the United States. From 1891 to the close of the century another 1,225,000 arrived and the total Catholic population grew to 12,041,000. From 1901 through 1910 the number of Catholic newcomers was almost 2,320,000 and the total Catholic population leaped to 16,336,000. In a brief two-decade period the Roman Catholic numbers had been increased by more than 7.3 million.

After the end of the First World War there were 20 million Catholics in the country. Immigration virtually ended in 1924, but despite that fact an amazing growth in American Catholicism came after the Second World War, when the number of communicants jumped from a little over 24 million in 1945 to almost double that figure by 1970. Altogether, in a period of 180 years, from 1790 to 1970, the Catholic Church increased the number of its American members from 30,000 to approximately 47.8 million.

When the twentieth century began, the Catholic Church had already established eighty-two dioceses, with some twelve thousand priests and about forty men's religious societies, as well as more than 250 sisterhoods, most of which were of European origin. Inevitably, during this growth there was also a gradual acquisition of property by Catholic clergy, so that by the first decades of the twentieth century the amount of Church property had reached an extraordinary scale. Before the First World War, Catholic jurisdictions in the United States were on a mission status and received financial aid from mission-aid societies in Germany, Austria and France, but by 1920 American Catholics were making increasing contributions of their own to Rome. Long before the Wall Street crash of 1929, the Catholic Church had established itself as the largest single religious body in North America—and the richest.

Viewing the dollar value of Catholic churches and rectories, one notes that in 1850 the total worth of these types of structure came to $9.3 million. Subsequent figures: 1870, $60.9 million; 1890, $118.3 million; 1906, $292.6 million; 1916, $435.5 million; 1936, $891.4 million. The foregoing figures, which do not include church-owned hospitals, schools, cemeteries and other facilities, are from statistics compiled by the U. S. Census Bureau, which discontinued this category after 1936.

Just as extraordinary as the growth of Catholic numbers was the expansion of the educational operations of the Catholic Church in the United States. By 1921 there were already about 6,550 Catholic elementary schools, 1,552 high schools, 43 colleges for men and 24 colleges for women—with a total attendance exceeding 2 million. A quarter of a century later the Catholic Church owned, controlled and supervised a grand total of 11,075 educational establishments, which were providing instruction for more than 3.2 million students.

There were, in 1945, more than 14,500 parishes, upward of 13,400 men in the religious orders and nearly 180,000 women who had joined the sisterhood.

Shortly after the end of the First World War, Westchester County in New York State underwrote a detailed study of the historical origin of the exemption of charitable institutions from taxes. One of the first complete studies ever attempted of the actual property exempt in a given county, it explained the situation for Westchester during the years 1919 and 1920. It made the point that Westchester's tax problem "is symptomatic of the tax problem of all counties throughout the state and for that matter all counties throughout the country." Later, during the mid-'20s, Edith MacFadden did a detailed study of Massachusetts and the other forty-seven states, using data she got from the offices of tax commissioners across the country. She reported that the tax-exempt property had increased in each of the three years covered by the report— in 1924 by $94.6 million, in 1925 by $50.5 million, and in 1926 by $60 million.

Studies of church property and tax exemptions began to appear with more frequency around the time of the American depression. Most of these were carried out by state or city commissions. In a 1933 study for New York State, John G. Saxe quoted figures that showed that the taxable property in 1919 was $12.6 billion and the exempt property the same year was $2.9 billion. Prior to the depression, in the year 1927, the taxable property was put at $25 billion, whereas the exempt property was then $4.6 billion.

In 1926 the U. S. Census Bureau tabulated urban and rural churches separately for the first time. Not mentioned in the listings of church properties, however, were colleges, seminaries, cemeteries, hospitals, parsonages, parish halls, publishing houses, extra land and a wide range of commercial properties and investments. With 202,930 churches reporting, the total property value came to $3.8 billion. The Catholic Church was first, with a figure of $837,271,053; the Methodists were in second place with $406 million. Under the listed expenditures, the total for all churches was reported as more than $817 million. The Catholic churches listed the highest rate of expenditure, the figure being $204.5 million (25 percent of the total).

In 1936 the Census Bureau made some changes in the procedure for the previous period. A total of 173,754 churches (fewer than the 1926 number) reported total value of church edifices as $3.4 billion. Once again the Catholics led, with their total value placed at $787,001,357, followed by the Methodists with $345.4 million. In that particular census 45,376 churches reported indebtedness. The largest number of churches reporting debts were Catholic; a total of 6,996 Catholic churches had debts that reached a figure of $189,350,733, or 37.2 percent of the total indebtedness for all churches. Nearly 95 percent of the churches reported on their operating expenses in 1936, and once again the Catholic churches were in the lead, reporting expenses that came to $139,073,358, or 26.8 percent of the amount for all churches.*

Catholic figures for 1968 show 30 archdioceses, 123 dioceses, 18,064 parishes, 23,734 churches, 4,346 missions, 1,404 stations, and 12,694 chapels. The compilation also shows 788 hospitals, 239 orphanages and asylums, 420 homes for the aged, 124 seminaries (with 39,838 enrollees), 305 colleges and universities (with 433,960 students), and 13,030 elementary and secondary schools (with some 5 million pupils). In addition, mention should be made of the vast complex of rectories, correctional institutions, publishing facilities, nunneries, convents, monasteries, diocesan headquarters, etc. As for Church personnel, it can be reported that at the end of 1968 there

* 1936 was the last year the United States Census Bureau collected and made available information for the above categories.

were nearly 60,000 priests, some 12,260 brothers, and more than 176,000 sisters.

In tracing the economic growth of the Catholic Church in the United States, however briefly, it should be evident that the Church is one of the great success stories in American annals. The growth of the Church in Canada has been equally impressive.

Catholic history in Canada dates from the foundation of Quebec in 1608 by Samuel de Champlain. A few years later the first missionaries, the Jesuits and the Franciscan Récollects, began to arrive. Though mainly working among some 100,-000 Indians, these two groups of missionary priests also provided some pastoral care for the French settlers. The first women's religious communities in Canada were established between 1637 and 1658. Ecclesiastical organization began with the appointment of François de Montmorency Laval as vicar apostolic of New France in 1658. In 1674 Quebec became the first diocese in the territory.

The English acquired possession of Canada, and of seventy thousand French-speaking inhabitants, through the Treaty of Paris in 1763. English–French and Anglican–Catholic differences and tensions sprang up, and at first the British government refused to recognize the titles of Catholic Church officials, hindered the clergy in their work and attempted to institute a non-Catholic educational system. Laws were passed in 1774, however, guaranteeing religious and civil liberties to Catholics. During the fifteen years following, new communities of men's and women's religious groups began to join those already in the country. Missionaries of the Oblates of Mary Immaculate contributed to the penetration of the West, where new jurisdictions were established. Meanwhile, a Catholic school system underwent a period of substantial growth, and in 1886 Canada had its first cardinal. Early in the twentieth century Canada had twenty-three dioceses, 3,500 priests, 2.4

million Catholics, about thirty men's religious orders and seventy women's. The highest concentration of Catholics was to be found in the eastern portion, just as it is today.

The official statistics for Canada, based on 1969 figures (the latest available), show that there are over 8.7 million Catholics in the country out of a population of 20.7 million. Canada has seventeen archdioceses, forty-six dioceses and 6,063 parishes and missions. There are also 14,758 priests, 65,315 members of women's orders and 12,655 members of men's orders.

Intimately woven into Canada's Catholic history is the name of an Indian girl, Katherine or Kateri Tekakwitha, the "Lily of the Mohawks," who should be mentioned in passing. At the age of eighteen Kateri became the first Mohawk Indian to be baptized in the Catholic rites. This did not go well with her uncle, Chief Odegongo, who had raised her from the age of four. Partially out of revenge, Odegongo commissioned a young Mohawk buck to deflower the girl, who had taken vows of chastity. The young warrior did not succeed, because Kateri drove him off with an ax, an act that made her a national Catholic heroine. After finding her place among the Iroquois Indians who lived along the St. Lawrence River, Kateri took up her work in the Jesuit missionary school. She died in 1680 at the age of twenty-four, but in her brief life she had introduced Christianity to her people under very hostile circumstances. Though her name is virtually unknown in the United States, the Tekakwitha grave site at Caughnawaga, Canada, has become a pilgrimage center for North American Indians. The Lily of the Mohawks is now being considered for sainthood, and if she is canonized, she will be the first American Indian to have been so honored.

3

THEY HAVE THEIR ORDERS

The people of this country are . . . jealous . . . of the wealth which has been piled up by no effort at all . . .
—GEORGE WASHINGTON

THE CRACK of an auctioneer's gavel brought an end to a rags-to-riches story the likes of which Texas may never see again. In a move to help pay off $3 million in debts, Mr. and Mrs. Ernest Medders, who had borrowed from an order of nuns almost $2 million at the rate of $40,000 a month, put their major possessions under the auctioneer's hammer. The event drew several thousand people to Muenster, Texas, the small cattle town about sixty miles northwest of Dallas where, in a mansion the Medderses had built on a rocky farm, the couple had thrown some of the biggest, most expensive parties Texas had ever known—all with money lent to them by the Poor Sisters of St. Francis Seraph of the Perpetual Adoration, which has its headquarters in Mishawaka, Indiana.

To lend Mr. Medders this money, the Sisters had to draw on funds allocated to them by the United States government for twelve hospitals their order owned in Indiana, Illinois, Kentucky, Ohio and Tennessee. The money the Poor Sisters asked for and received from the federal till came to exactly $11,637,034. Without asking any collateral, the Poor Sisters speculated on Mr. Medders, who believed himself to be an heir to a Texas oil field worth $500 million and who had promised, as a practicing Roman Catholic, to be a generous contributor to the order's welfare in life and death. The gamble did not pay off.

The saga of the Medderses started in Memphis, Tennessee, in 1961. Ernest Medders, an illiterate, was then fifty-one years old and was working as a mechanic's helper for the Gulf Oil Refinery at fifty dollars a week. His wife, Margaret, had a job as a practical nurse at Memphis' St. Joseph Hospital. The couple lived in a low-rent housing project with their ten children. To help keep the wolf from the door, Ernest often sold vegetables from the back of his station wagon parked alongside the highways. One day news reached Mr. Medders that a lawyer in Mississippi had initiated legal action on behalf of three thousand people who believed they owned a share in one of the biggest oil pools in the world, the famed Spindletop petroleum field in Texas. Included in the list was the name of Ernest Medders. His reaction to all this was that he was the sole heir and that he would win the $500 million field for himself. Sharing Ernest's belief, Margaret forthwith let everybody at work know that her husband would soon become heir to this large sum of money.

To press his claim, Ernest needed funds. One thing led to another, and because the Poor Sisters ran the St. Joseph Hospital where Mrs. Medders had been a faithful and trustworthy employee, the mother superior advanced Margaret's husband the sum of $500. This was followed by a second loan of $60,-000. Ernest and Margaret and their ten children moved to Texas and bought a house at Muenster. A year later they also acquired a 185-acre farm for $57,000, and on it they built a fifteen-room brick house and a pool. The price of this estate, including the furnishings and the landscaping, eventually reached $250,000. Every penny of this money came from the Poor Sisters, who were now depositing $40,000 every month into the Medderses' account as a loan.

Ernest, who kept close tabs on his lawyers' suit for the Spindletop millions, then went into cattle raising. He stocked his ranch with a good herd of registered Black Angus and Red Angus cattle and fine Appaloosa horses. Not one to stint on expenses, he then hired a Dallas public-relations firm to give his ranch, a showplace known as Colonial Acres Farm, a better image. At the same time, Mrs. Medders opened an account at the Neiman-Marcus department store and began making purchases at the rate of about $2,000 a month. She even hired a full-time hairdresser and set up a complete shop at Colonial Acres where she and her house guests could have their hair done. And so that her daughters would not have to live in a dorm while at finishing school in Dallas, Mrs. Medders purchased a $40,000 house for them next door to the school.

By this time Ernest and Margaret Medders had begun to spread their social wings. They started throwing fabulous caviar-cum-champagne-cum-orchestra parties, and word of their elaborate fetes spread quickly. At a fund-raising dance for which Guy Lombardo and his Royal Canadians supplied the music, Mrs. Medders underwrote all the costs and invited Lombardo, the band and a hundred other guests to stay after the ball for a midnight breakfast. She followed this up by staging another party for a thousand people in a mammoth new barn that was large enough to hold a rodeo—as it did from time to time. She made publicity capital out of this shindig by getting her press agent to con a Dallas television station into doing a Special on the event. The press agent went her one better: he invited newspaper executives to come as guests, and the Medderses got big writeups in all the papers. To bring people in from Dallas, the magnanimous couple hired buses with built-in bars and plenty of whiskey and champagne. Guests from other cities were flown to nearby Gainesville in chartered planes and were then ferried by helicopter to Colonial Acres. The pilot of the helicopter wore, it should come as no surprise, a tuxedo and a top hat. What was most impressive about this party, perhaps, was the champagne constantly flowing from the ranch's central fountain. This sort of touch was only the beginning, for the Medderses outdid even themselves as time went on.

For instance, they once hired a special train with six coaches and a band to bring their daughters' classmates from Dallas to the ranch. Another time they paid for radio ads every hour on the hour to wish their friends season's greetings for Christmas and New Year's. Once they gave a ball in honor of Mrs. Jeane Dixon, the Washington clairvoyant. Then there was the super-lavish wedding of their oldest son, not to mention a 4-H horse show for twelve hundred kids at the ranch, a mammoth party in Memphis for Angus breeders, and a charity ball for a crippled children's organization. While Mrs. Medders was charging an $80,000 necklace, a $75,000 mink coat and a $65,000 ring at Neiman-Marcus, Mr. Medders was busy borrowing money adding up to $730,000 from banks in Muenster, Wichita Falls and Memphis to push his cattle business.

Meanwhile, the show-offy largesse that included His and Hers Cadillacs did not escape the attention of the bigshots in the Texas capital or those in Washington. Texas Governor John B. Connally and his attorney general were guests at the ranch. Ernest and Margaret Medders eventually came to know President Lyndon B. Johnson. He invited them as part of a select group to the White House for a reception where they met Secretary of State Dean Rusk, who drove them to a cocktail party at the Mexican Embassy. President Johnson had the Medderses and seven other couples come into his living quarters in the White House for a late dinner after the reception and for a movie in his private theater. Mr. Johnson gave the couple a photograph of himself signed "As ever, Lyndon B. Johnson," and, since he was flying to Texas the next day, he invited Ernie and Maggie to accompany him on the presidential jet, Air Force One.

Just how long Mr. and Mrs. Medders could continue living and spending like characters out of Edna Ferber's *Giant* was anybody's guess. As it happened, the end came suddenly, soon after it was reported that President Johnson had given Mrs. Medders a peck on the cheek, a moment she described as "the most thrilling event of my life." It seems that the Poor Sisters had a change in administration, and the new mother superior, apprehensive about all the publicity and hoopla the Medderses had created, took a dim view of the monthly $40,000 loan her organization was meting out. She stopped the money payment to the Medderses. And with that the bottom fell out.

While hotels, florists, caterers, liquor dealers and sundry other creditors began getting nervous over nonpayment of debts, some of the Medderses' relatives, rankled by the couple's press notices and beginning to suspect that Cousin Ernie had somehow gotten his hands on the Spindletop inheritance and cut them out, filed suit to force him to disclose the source of his income. In court he explained that all of his funds had come by way of loans from the Poor Sisters and from banks. That broke the bubble, and in May 1967 Ernest Medders, Esq., filed for bankruptcy. The Poor Sisters, declining to press any charges, did not try to recover their loss. They had been bilked for exactly $1,940,000.

One of the curious things about religious orders—and the aforementioned Poor Sisters are no exception—is that they usually start out by being poor and eventually become either well-to-do or just plain rich. Paradoxically, though individual members of an order do keep their vows of poverty, the property owned by the order becomes bigger and bigger as a matter of normal economics. This is an almost inevitable occurrence, in view of the fact that they are spared most forms of taxation. The irony is that society finds itself with religious professionals who are dedicated to perpetual poverty living often in better circumstances than the poor people of their state or country—with better food, better clothes, better housing and fewer fears about being put through an economic wringer.

One way to understand the setup of the American Catholic Church is to compare it to a military organization—its various regiments and companies led by commanding officers of ranked degrees of authority, each subject to the supreme authority of the commander in chief, the Pope. As an adjunct to this structure are the religious orders, which range from such historic groups as the Jesuits, the Franciscans, the Dominicans and the Benedictines to other, lesser-known societies created in recent years. The part played by these religious orders is a substantial one, both in terms of their spiritual, moral and intellectual work and in terms of their financial operations. It must be remembered, confusing as it may be, that although all the Catholic orders are part and parcel of the pontifical hierarchy, they function in the United States (as elsewhere in the world) with virtual autonomy in their special areas. Each order has its own rules and charters granted at the time of its foundation from Rome.

Shielding their members from the temptation of the world, the religious orders adopt a manner of living that is narrow and deeply devotional. Every order has its governing hierarchy, its monasteries and convents and its systems of discipline. Poverty, chastity and obedience are the watchwords. The head of each order is eager to recruit more members for his organization and to promote the welfare and prosperity of the community. In general the work of these orders is mainly concerned with education and charity, social services and the care of people—orphans, the sick, the elderly, etc.

Despite their freedom to rule and run themselves—often answering to no one, not even the local archbishop—within the jurisdiction of a diocese in which they are physically located, the religious orders must render financial accounts to the Holy See every five years. And at stated intervals they can usually be made to give an accounting to a local bishop, who in no case can make demands of their money for projects outside the realm of the given order. However, women's religious orders technically do not have full freedom on matters of money. When nuns' organizations want to make investments, be they community funds or money from gifts or dowries, they are required to consult a male officer of the Church who has jurisdictional authority. In contracting debts of more than $6,000, religious orders—both men's and women's—must get the written consent of their superiors or a ranking officer from their nearest chancery, if not from the archbishop himself. Apparently this was done by the Poor Sisters who lent money to the Medderses. Although it is likely that they were warned, as are other religious orders, not to run their organization into debt, the warning does not seem to have achieved the desired effect.

As another manifestation of corporate spiritual life, there has sprung up within the past fifty years a new type of order known as the secular institute. These institutes are societies of men and women who "dedicate themselves to God in perfect charity." Taking vows to be obedient to superiors of their institute and to practice poverty, members pursue their own professions and earn their own livelihood, which they devote to serving others and spreading their faith. It should be pointed out that the Vatican did not give full recognition and approval to these secular institutes until February 1947, when Pope Pius XII issued his "Provida Mater Ecclesia" statement.

As for the religious institutes, there are in the United States nearly seventy such organizations for men and over four hundred for women, most of them worldwide in scope. Perhaps the most economically powerful and certainly the largest of these orders is the Society of Jesus. Of the world's 35,500 Jesuits, about 7,500 are Americans, and they form the most vigorous segment of the order.

Although the Jesuits are an order of the Catholic Church, they are neither friars nor monks. They do not live in monasteries. In the United States they dress like all other priests. The Jesuits run houses of retreat, publish intellectual periodicals, service Catholic parish churches and administer a great string of schools, the best known of which are Fordham University, Marquette University, St. Louis University, Boston College and Loyola University of Chicago. Altogether they have jurisdiction over some 120,000 students in twenty-eight universities, forty-three high schools, thirteen law schools, ten nursing schools, eight schools of engineering, five schools of medicine and a foreign-service school. The teaching of young people, however, is not their primary interest in the United States. The Society of Jesus qualifies as a power in international finance, and the American wing of this order qualifies it as one of the most awesome of all Catholic organizations involved in commercial enterprises.

With headquarters in Rome, just outside the borders of Vatican City, the Jesuits—who are over 435 years old—have ten "provinces" in the United States. Horizontally, the order is divided into three main categories—priests, lay brothers and future priests (the last-named require fifteen years of formal training). Just as the idea of obedience is a trademark of the Jesuits, so too is the vow of poverty. As a mendicant order living off alms, the Jesuits incorporate austerity as a part of their life. A Jesuit personally is not allowed to own anything. Whatever he may own before taking his vows he has to discard when he becomes a full member of the order. If he earns any money on the outside, he must turn it over to his superiors; he is, however, allotted a modest sum for his needs. While the poverty requirement may be imposed on the individuals within the order, the Jesuits collectively do not practice poverty, for money is part of their bone structure. In fact, they are, paradoxically, the wealthiest of all the Catholic organizations with the exception of the Vatican itself.

Like all other Catholic business operations, the Jesuits shroud their money in secrecy. From time to time there have been assertions made about Jesuit wealth and Jesuit investments. While some of the claims found in anti-Catholic publications are exaggerated, others are not. One thing is certain: the Jesuits rarely engage in denials of their financial resources or ask their so-called accusers to print retractions. A reasonable estimate of the Jesuits' annual American income is approximately $250 million. This figure does not include the substantial educational subsidies given the Jesuits by the U.S. government for some of their institutions.

Schooled in the Vatican style of poker, the Jesuits know how to shuffle the cards in such a way that dealing from the bottom is not necessary. There was, for example, the time in 1962 when the Veterans Administration classified the Hines Veterans Administration Hospital, a $6.3-million structure standing on sixty-one acres of valuable land just outside Chicago, as surplus and gave it at no cost to the Jesuit Fathers of Loyola University. A year after the transfer, the V.A. found it was short of medical facilities in the area and would have to build another hospital at a cost of $18.5 million. During the ensuing investigation, it was learned that the administrator of veterans' affairs who had declared the Hines hospital as surplus was a devout Roman Catholic serving as a member of the advisory board of Loyola University. Although some demands were made for a full-blown Congressional investigation, pressures were exerted on the majority leaders of the House and the Senate to let the matter die. Which it did.

The Jesuits have a financial interest in four of America's largest aircraft-manufacturing plants—Lockheed, Curtiss-Wright, Douglas and Boeing. They also have a participation —but not a controlling interest, as the German press has reported—in the Phillips Oil Company, on which they keep a closer financial eye. The American wing of the Society of Jesus also has invested heavily in both Republic and National Steel. Thanks to guidance and help from the Jesuits, the Vatican has acquired stock in such companies as the Goodyear Tire & Rubber Company, Firestone, U. S. Rubber, the Baltimore & Ohio Railroad, the Rock Island line, the Missouri Pacific Railroad and the Erie line. Other companies include the Montana Power Company, Indiana Electric, Oklahoma Gas & Electric, American Commonwealth Power, Texas Electric, and Pacific Gas & Electric. Also included are the Pillsbury Flour Company, the Lane Bryant department store in New York City, the Washington Silk Company and the Atlantic City Convention Hall.

Outright Jesuit ownership of a company is nearly always impossible to pin down, given the supreme secrecy that invariably attends these operations. But the Jesuits have never hidden the fact that their Loyola University in New Orleans owns a television station, WWL-TV, and radio station WWL-AM and -FM. Though operating as a profit-making enterprise, the two stations enjoy a tax-free status, a fact that rankles its closest competitor, WDSU-TV. A spokesman for WDSU-TV said that the Jesuit stations, which charge $325 a minute for a television commercial during the prime evening hours, fifty dollars less than the rival station, earn an annual profit in excess of $2 million. The money that they do not disburse in tax payments, he said, is used to pay for ads in magazines like *TV Guide*. This, in turn, brings WWL-TV additional advertising clientele and therefore more revenue. Moreover, by not having to pay taxes, the Jesuit stations are able to maintain their ad rates at a lower base than their competitors.

The Jesuits are also active in commercial real-estate enterprises. This too is kept a top secret. Just how extensive their landholdings are could not be determined by this writer, because all too often a Jesuit-owned parcel of land is hidden behind the name of a private individual acting for the order. However, disclosures are made from time to time. For instance, when Resortland, Inc., wanted to build an array of exclusive homes with a private golf course and swimming pool, the company sought to purchase 850 acres of prime land six miles from Leonardtown in southern Maryland. The sale for $1 million was finally completed with the owner, the Society of Jesus.

In matters of business, the Jesuits often act as a pressure group. Late in 1969, when Congress was considering a bill that put a tax on the profits of all unrelated businesses operated by churches and religious orders, the Jesuits got busy and applied some pressure. Although the bill was passed and signed into law by President Nixon, they were successful in getting the Senate to add an amendment which allowed the profits in question a period of six untaxed months. It also got the Senate to include the provision that no income tax be applied "to a religious order or to an educational institution maintained by such a religious order . . . which provides services under licenses issued by a federal regulatory agency for ten years or more . . ." This pressure was applied through Senator Russell B. Long of Louisiana, chairman of the Senate Finance Committee, because the Jesuits wanted to keep the tax exemption for their profitable radio and TV stations.

But what is considered the most important Jesuit business affiliation concerns the Bank of America. In order to better understand just what connection the Society of Jesus has with it, let us examine a bit of the history of this, the largest bank in the world.

The story of the Bank of America is closely related to the story of its founder, Amadeo Peter Giannini. One morning in the year 1906 Mr. Giannini was awakened at his home outside San Francisco to receive the shocking news that an earthquake had almost destroyed the city. "People are wandering the streets in a daze and they've lost everything," he was told. To this Mr. Giannini growled, "Not our depositors!" The young banker then loaded $2 million in bills and coins onto a vegetable wagon and pushed his way into the still-burning city. Setting himself up a few feet from a building that was smoking rubble, Mr. Giannini paid off his depositors and made loans from a rickety table. It was unorthodox banking, but it was the big-brother style favored by Mr. Giannini. The informality and the friendliness of A. P. Giannini permeate the Bank of America today. Despite being a fiscal colossus, the Bank of America strives to overcome the curse by being a pal to the folks in California and every other state in the Union, as well as to the people of twenty-eight nations.

Bank of America will go to great lengths to make depositors happy. In San Francisco's Chinatown, for instance, the local branch keeps a few abacuses on some of the counters, since some of the people have more faith in the ancient counting gadget than in the electrified adding machines. Also, every one of the tellers and most of the branch officials speak Chinese. In another instance, when a Bank of America branch was formally opened in the Mexican district of Los Angeles, the local people came in to meet the Spanish-speaking employees and to eat tacos. The new building, carrying out the Mexican motif, had redwood ceilings and colorful tiled floors. The music coming from the loudspeakers had a Latin-American flavor.

According to the bank's annual report at the end of 1969, the total consolidated resources amounted to $25,573,116,000.

Deposits stood at more than $22 billion, and investments in securities surpassed the $4 billion mark. The net income for the year reached better than $152 million. In a midyear statement at the end of June 1970 BankAmerica reported a net income of over $73.5 million and total resources of more than $27.6 billion. During 1969, thirteen new Bank of America branches were opened, increasing to seventy-five the number of countries in which the bank serves. These figures are a far cry from the days when founder Giannini roamed the streets, knocking on doors to get clients for the bank he had founded in a one-room former saloon after borrowing $150,000 from friends.

When Mr. Giannini died in 1949, he left his estate, which totaled $489,000, to a foundation to provide scholarships for bank employees and for medical research. In his will, Mr. Giannini included the following statement: "Administer this trust generously and nobly, remembering always human suffering. Let no legal technicality, ancient precedent, or outmoded legal philosophy defeat the purpose of this trust. Like Saint Francis of Assisi, do good—do not merely theorize about goodness."

Mr. Giannini's "Christian" approach to banking may or may not be behind the constant rumors that the Jesuits own 51 percent of the Bank of America. In founding the Bank of America, Mr. Giannini was acting as an agent for the Jesuits, who, according to one report, were the friends who lent him the $150,000. In an article in *Playboy* magazine several years ago, Bishop James A. Pike, accepting the rumor at face value, estimated that the Society of Jesus realizes "a yearly income of $250 million" from its Bank of America holdings and many other investments. An official of the Bank of America went on record as saying that the allegations in *Playboy* were "completely untrue and without even a small basis of fact." "Our bank," the spokesman added, "has more than 200,000 stock-

holders holding a total of 28,480,000 shares, and no individual person or organization owns as much as one percent of our stock other than the 5 percent owned by a profit-sharing plan for employees of the bank."

Confronted with the problem of trying to pin down the truth about the Jesuit involvement in the Bank of America, this writer pursued the facts as far as it was possible. It is known that the Jesuits in the California province own 463 shares of BankAmerica stock, at a worth of about $25,000. The Jesuits in the state of Oregon own two hundred shares of BankAmerica stock, valued at approximately $12,000. There was no other information forthcoming as to what stocks the other eight Jesuit provinces in the United States have in the Bank of America, nor what interest the world headquarters in Rome retains in the same institution. If the Society of Jesus has any large holding of BankAmerica stock, it would doubtless be in the name of private persons or individual members of the order using their real names instead of their ecclesiastical names.

Whenever some information about Jesuit money comes to public light, myths begin to fly thither and yon about how much of a megafortune the Jesuits have. Such wild talk is inevitable. Yet despite this multiplicity of whispers, which breaks out from time to time, the Jesuits continue to damage their image by not making public declarations in the form of annual profit-and-loss statements. Rarely is anything ever reported about the internal finances of a Jesuit province, of which there are ten in the United States. Last year, however, the New York Province of the Society of Jesus, the largest one in America (with a total membership of nearly 1,300), elected to discuss rather openly some of its money problems, and it was revealed that the total receipts for the New York Province annually come to a figure approximating $1.6 million, of which nearly $650,000 comes from dividends and interest, approximately

$345,000 comes from the yearly taxes levied on the Jesuit communities of the province, and $80,000 comes from fundraising efforts. Gifts and legacies bring in another $125,000, and about $260,000 trickles in from various other endeavors. However, the New York Province in recent years has been showing an annual loss, its total expenditures reaching nearly $2.8 million. To cover the yearly deficits, the province, which is worth in the neighborhood of $15 to $20 million, has had to dip into its bank account for sums as high as $1 million.

Another Catholic organization which, like the Jesuits, has been subjected to a proliferation of whispers and gossip is the Knights of Columbus. Let us take a look at this "second-richest Catholic society."

The Knights of Columbus is a fraternal organization of Catholic men with a membership of nearly 1.2 million spread over the fifty states of the U. S., the ten provinces of Canada, Mexico and several other Latin-American countries. For more than a century, this society has offered to pay $25,000 to anybody who can furnish proof that an alleged "Bogus Oath" is subscribed to by its members.

The so-called "oath"—which has not been published on these pages for legal reasons, but which appeared in the *Congressional Record* of February 15, 1913, Volume 49, page 3219—speaks of "burning, hanging and strangling non-Catholic fellow Christians." Apparently an attempt on the part of some anti-Catholic persons to create prejudice against the Knights of Columbus, the "oath" has been published or otherwise circulated on more than one occasion. K. of C. officials have won convictions of criminal libel in California, Michigan, Georgia, New Jersey, Pennsylvania, Minnesota and Colorado when the scurrilous pledge has been printed.

The Knights of Columbus has been active in many apostolic and community programs since it was chartered as a fraternal benefit order in Connecticut in 1882. Since 1914 the group has

provided college educations for more than 1,200 students, granting scholarship aid valued at $3 million a year. In addition, the K. of C. has spent millions of dollars advertising in secular publications and on radio and television to counter what it believes is the communication media's focus on what is wrong with the Church rather than what is right with it. Every ad the K. of C. publishes reaches nearly 42 million homes in the U. S. and Canada and has a coupon which can be clipped by a reader who wants to have further information about the Church. With assets of $381,705,740 (as of audited account figures at the end of 1969, an increase of over $22.5 million from the previous year), the K. of C. runs an extensive insurance business for approximately a half-million subscribers and engages in a number of other money-making operations. Insurance currently in force surpasses the $1.84-billion mark. In January 1969, on the advice of its consulting actuaries, the Knights put into effect a substantial increase in the scale of dividends payable to the group's certificate holders; the amount set aside by dividends during 1969 reached a figure that was $7.8 million. The most recent figure available shows that the K. of C. has paid out well over $175 million in benefits to its clients since the society's modern insurance program went into force in 1940.

Some of the profits from the insurance program and from other business enterprises are invested by the Knights in diversified bonds representing 58 percent of its investment portfolio. The K. of C. invests about $100,000 a month in high-quality securities, as part of its common-stock program. Seventeen percent of the Knights' assets (a bit more than $65 million) is tied up in 154 mortgage loans to Catholic institutions. These assets produced a net investment income of over $15.6 million in 1968, an increase of 11 percent over 1967. During the first six months of 1969, the bond investments of this Catholic men's organization exceeded $10 million and

49

brought an average yield of 7 percent. The same percentage figure is the present rate of interest on the K. of C. church mortgages. Officials of the fraternity, taking cognizance of a daily revenue that exceeds $200,000, believe that these dollars should be working in the form of certificates of deposit and commercial paper; such short-term investments during 1968 brought over $190,000 to the society's treasury.

Although the Knights of Columbus makes these figures available to its membership, club officers are rather reluctant to reveal similar data about some of the other operations in which they have financial stakes. Apparently because no income taxes are paid on the commercial income derived from some of these properties, the organization prefers to keep this information to itself. It is known, however, that the K. of C. owns the Fuller Dry Goods Company property in St. Louis, the former New Haven Railroad headquarters building, the Brunswick-Balke-Collender Company building in Chicago, the site of the Sheraton Hotel in New Haven, Crucible Steel's Detroit warehouse, the steel tube mill of the Bridgeport Brass Company, the St. Louis Frontenac Apartments, and several large stores in Philadelphia and Camden, New Jersey.

The official publication of the Knights is another source of revenue. A well-edited monthly magazine, *Columbia* carries a healthy percentage of national advertising, has the largest circulation of any Catholic magazine and boasts a paid distribution of more than a million copies. Although no report is offered regarding *Columbia*'s solid finances, the magazine can be justified purely on the grounds that an impressive number of its articles are reprinted every year in other magazines, newspapers and pamphlets and quoted extensively by other communication media and by public speakers.

With a loan from the federal government, the Knights of Columbus built the Christopher Homes in Tucson, Arizona, in 1963 at a cost of $5 million. For this project the K. of C.

won a construction loan of $516,000, but effectuated only one payment on the mortgage. After the Knights had collected rents for some four years, Washington officers foreclosed, and in 1967 the University of Arizona acquired the property through purchase for $2.4 million. The federal government lost a total of nearly $4 million in this undertaking.

In another complicated transaction, the Knights bought for $6.5 million the land on which Yankee Stadium in New York stands, the adjoining parking lots and other nearby property, as well as the stadium of the New York Yankee baseball farm club in Kansas City, Missouri. At the outset a Chicago broker purchased the New York land from the Yankee owners for the K. of C. and then quickly resold the property of the Knights (the operation of Yankee Stadium itself was not affected by the sale). The owners of Yankee Stadium signed long leases with the Knights, who invested a reported sum of $2.5 million for the land alone. From this investment the K. of C. receives $182,000 each year on a lease that runs twenty-eight years, with renewal options for another forty-two years. The Knights will realize about $1 million in profits from this transaction and, according to the terms of the contract, will eventually come into full possession of the Yankee Stadium structure itself.

Thus when, in October 1965, Pope Paul went to New York City to visit the United Nations and later presided at a pontifical Mass in Yankee Stadium, His Holiness in effect was on home grounds.

4

FISCAL FITNESS

No one is opposed to sensible and reasonable profits, but as between profits first and humanity afterwards and humanity first and profits afterwards, we have no reason for hesitation.
—FRANKLIN D. ROOSEVELT

SEVERAL YEARS AGO when a hundred newspaper reporters and a battery of television cameramen were called to a press conference during a meeting in Washington of the National Conference of Catholic Bishops, they were presented a rather unique surprise. As they gathered in the briefing room, the newsmen expected to be given a hot story on the day's behind-closed-doors discussion of a report recommending limited disclosure of financial records. Instead, Bishop James P. Shannon, auxiliary at St. Paul–Minneapolis, faced the eager press corps and said simply, "There is nothing to report from this morning's meeting. Now if anybody has a deck of cards, I'll do some tricks for you."

That morning the bishops had indeed taken up the delicate matter of whether the Catholic dioceses throughout the United States should issue yearly statements on their fiscal state. But they had voted to keep their discussion a secret and to disclose nothing about the meeting to the press. Thus the total news blackout.

In November 1969, the Catholic bishops, meeting once again in Washington, approved a proposal to set up a uniform system of accounting in dioceses, though the system was not to be totally binding. The sum of $57,000 was set aside to hire an accounting firm which would lay down the guidelines whereby ranking priests could disclose the financial conditions of their particular jurisdictions. The bishops' decision to open Catholic Church accounting, however, has not brought an end to the controversy among the top echelons of the American Catholic Church.

Some members of the top clergy believe that since parishioners help support a diocese, they have a "right" to know how their money is being used. The opposition is firm in its belief that the more you tell people, the more people will want to know. Their feeling is that the reports would open up individual financial transactions to public scrutiny and criticism. Others also warn that the present credit ratings of most Catholic dioceses are good but that these could change if financial statements began appearing. In a report late in 1968, the then Bishop Terence Cooke, as chairman of the Bishops' Diocesan Financial Statement Committee, recommended that dioceses consider giving financial statements but not full statements. These statements, he added, should be provided in the form of essay-type reports rather than as accounting sheets. Objecting to the Cooke report, one group of bishops said that the listing of assets and particularly of real estate, which at best would be vague approximations, would lead to "uninformed speculation" by Catholics and non-Catholics alike.

If the money question is a live issue among the bishops, it is equally controversial among the communicants themselves. The National Association of Laymen, which has twelve thousand members in twenty-nine chapters around the country, has demanded a public accountability. Dennis Landis, N.A.L. president, says his organization wants exposure of all information that would help laymen "make intelligent judgments about whether the Church is accomplishing her mission." Mr. Landis has pointed out that annual fund drives suffer because the secrecy surrounding Church finances leads to endless exaggeration about "what the Church really owns."

Despite the raging controversy, some Catholic jurisdictions have lifted the curtain by publishing financial statements. Aside from having aroused a certain skepticism as to their honesty or accuracy, the reports seem to have caused little or no commotion. Many of them are not really financial statements in the traditional sense but merely statements which disclose some financial information and which are essentially only the tip of an accounting iceberg. The reports do, however, reflect the individual priests' views on the question of whether or not to "open the books."

Although it is impossible to get an overall picture of a diocese's business affairs from these statements, they do give clues as to the size and scope of diocesan work and financial operations. With the exception of a report issued by the Pittsburgh Diocese, none of the figures in the reports gathered for this book were attested to by an independent accounting house. Yet several of the reports, offering excuses for inadequacies and shortcomings, stated that the reason for the relatively limited information was that a number of complicated accounting problems were involved in the preparation. It should also be noted that almost all the reports tended to show a bleak view of the financial state of the diocese.

The first financial report issued by the Archdiocese of Baltimore, for instance, concluded that its losses at the middle of June 1969 would come to $1.5 million. The Archbishop, Lawrence J. Cardinal Shehan, explained that the deficit would be met from a $4.3-million reserve fund accumulated over a period of years. In the city of Baltimore the Archbishop is in the process of phasing out the $900,000 annual subsidies to all five of the Catholic high schools.

Other figures cited in the Baltimore Archdiocese report show income at $2,777,436—with $1.3 million coming from the Catholic Charity Fund Appeal, $860,000 from the archdiocesan tax from parishes, $397,790 from investment and parish note income, $75,700 from rental income, $21,280 from fees paid to the archdiocesan chancery office, $25,000 from gifts and bequests, and $72,666 from cash on hand from the previous fiscal year. Three sources of income were not included in the operating budget: about $10 million collected in the Cardinal's Campaign for Charity and Education, which began in mid-1966; funds deposited in the chancery office by parishes (these are loans made to the archdiocese which pay the parishes 5 percent interest); and legacies to the archdiocese. Of the $10 million in the Cardinal's Campaign, better than $7.8 million has been spent to construct new facilities for the Little Sisters of the Poor, the House of the Good Shepherd and St. Elizabeth's School for Special Education of the mentally retarded. The remaining $2.2 million was spent to pay for construction of Catholic high schools. Expenditures, which came to $3,801,861, included $2.5 million for operation of twenty-eight offices, $1 million for the archdiocese's department of education, $100,000 for the Hope Program, and $100,000 for the Resource Bank. A high-school deficit of $885,638 was cited; this amount constituted the cost of running the schools over and above the tuition fees collected.

The Baltimore Archdiocese reported that the total value of all its property that was used for religious purposes was about $40 million, that its assets (including about $12 million in stocks and bonds) totaled $52,397,708, that its liabilities were $13,959,468 and that the net worth of tangibles was $29,162,-490. However, in 1968 when Dr. Martin A. Larson (whose research I have cited in other sections of this book) checked the tax rolls of Baltimore, he found that the assessed valuation of exempt Roman Catholic Church property within the city limits came to more than $81.6 million. His careful and extensive analyses showed that the assessments were actually not over 55 percent of fair market value, which therefore means that the actual worth of the Catholic property was more than $150 million. Dr. Larson showed that the Cathedral of Mary Our Queen had a replacement value of not less than $10 million. There were also seventy city parish churches, which had fifty-nine attached schools, cumulatively worth many more millions of dollars. This is not to mention an array of colleges, seminaries, diocesan high schools and hospitals. Baltimore's four Catholic hospitals, assessed at nearly $13 million, had a replacement value of at least $25 million, according to the Larson calculations. Loyola College, as another example, carried an assessment of approximately $2.3 million but reported a book value of nearly $6.8 million—with an actual value exceeding $10 million. Notre Dame College, assessed at $3 million, had a reported book value of more than $12.1 million and a replacement value of not less than $20 million.

Explaining that his statistics covered only the city itself and that the archdiocesan budget statement included sixty-five parishes outside the city, Dr. Larson added: "Since these 65 parishes include the most affluent areas with new churches and schools, there can be little doubt that assets outside the city roughly equal those within its borders. We come, therefore, to the conclusion that the true value of Roman Catholic exempt real estate alone in the Baltimore Archdiocese is not $40 million but nearly $400 million. . . ." *

Perhaps the most complete diocesan budget is the one pub-

* Martin A. Larson and C. Stanley Lowell, *Praise the Lord for Tax Exemption* (Washington and New York: Robert B. Luce, Inc., 1969), Chapter 5, Section III.

lished by Bishop Robert E. Tracy of Baton Rouge, Louisiana, the first Catholic clergyman in the country to issue a detailed financial statement. His report in September 1967 made national headlines and was reported on in the weekly news magazines. The diocesan report issued in September 1969 by Bishop Tracy ran the length of four tabloid-size newspaper pages and left, apparently, no questions about the operations of the Diocese of Baton Rouge. Bishop Tracy even added a postscript at the conclusion of his report in which he said he gladly welcomed and would print in the diocesan newspaper "any appropriate comment, favorable or unfavorable, which any of our priests, brothers, sisters and lay members of the diocese may choose to write in." Appearing as a supplement in the diocesan weekly paper and distributed to 33,000 subscribers, the September 1969 statement showed an income of $1,443,100 for the fiscal year of 1968. A summary of expenditures follows: interparochial schools, $843,800; seminaries, $181,100; special education, $46,300; school board, $43,500; department of religious education, $14,700; university apostolate, $129,100. The total expenditures for education reached $1,258,500. In the health and welfare division the figures showed: social services, $73,000; infirm priests' plan, $23,200; bishops' relief fund, $20,000; family life bureau, $17,700; youth activities, $15,500; support of other health and welfare activities, $103,300. Other expenditures included $542,400 for specialized services and $18,400 for support of pastoral activities. The Baton Rouge diocesan assets total $44.2 million, and the diocese's standing debt of approximately $3 million is being retired at the rate of 11 percent a year.

On the other hand, the Archdiocese of St. Paul–Minneapolis ended the 1968 year with a deficit totaling $422,597, after having also operated in the red for 1967. In the first financial report ever made by the archdiocese, Coadjutor Archbishop Leo C. Byrne revealed assets totaling $21.3 million. Not included in the report were the finances of 223 parishes (which operate 152 elementary schools), twenty-two high schools, two colleges, three seminaries, and other institutions including Catholic Welfare and Catholic Youth Center. The combined assets of the exclusions total millions of dollars and are administered independently. Bishop Byrne's report, therefore, covered only the finances and properties directly under the administration of the chancery, the central diocesan corporation. It showed that of the $1.4 million income received, a total of $906,595 came from annual parish assessments. Of the balance, $338,887 was accrued from special collections and gifts, while $176,492 was realized from investment income. Total disbursements were put at $1.8 million.

Property assessment accounted for some $14 million of the St. Paul–Minneapolis Archdiocese's $21 million in assets. The assets also included $3.5 million in restricted and dedicated funds, $1.3 million in endowment funds, $750,000 in the revolving-fund loan fund, $693,085 in the revolving expansion fund and $478,275 in general current funds. Except for the property funds, most of the assets are invested in marketable securities. In addition to owning five expansion sites of about twenty acres apiece, which will be used as possible locations for new parishes, the archdiocese owns five tracts of property in various parts of the Twin Cities metropolitan area, including one of seventy-seven acres in the suburban Cottage Grove neighborhood. The cemetery office reported assets of more than $5 million, spread over five cemeteries in which some 170,000 persons are buried. During the fiscal year a site that the archdiocese had acquired in 1950 for an additional cemetery was sold because the land was not considered satisfactory for burial purposes.

The Buffalo Diocese was another chancery which reported a deficit at year's end. Its net losses for 1968 were put at $847,-563. This represented an impressive improvement over the preceding year, when the diocese showed a net loss of $7.9 million. The operations showed assessments of $301,073 collected from parishes, use of $763,765 in Catholic Charities campaign money, and $401,254 in interest income, bequests and other revenues. Total general diocesan revenue for that year was $1.5 million. Against this were $2 million in expenditures for other educational, social, welfare, spiritual and general purposes. The diocese's operating loss was $538,811. Interest on debts amounted to $769,675. Central to the negative financial picture was a $1.2-million deficit, largely a result of the diocese's high-school operation.

The Diocese of Savannah, Georgia, issued a financial report in 1967 that gave every figure down to the last penny. It showed a net profit of $4,262.32, after citing a total income of $710,637.65 and total expenditures of $706,375.33. During that year the Savannah Diocese acquired two parcels of land and made due payment on another for a total of $13,635.50. Most of the income came from collections and gifts ($156,-548.36), interest on savings and dividends and interest on loans to parishes ($33,288.71), and parish assessments ($49,-152.11). Major expenses included salaries that totaled $33,-670.40, capital investments in seven parish operations that reached a figure of $248,000, and an education debt retirement that came to a figure of $120,773.47. Welfare costs were put at $66,715.85.

Revealing a deficit of $6,146 during 1968, the Diocese of Tucson, Arizona, reported an income of $1,614,298, expenses of $1,620,444 and an indebtedness exceeding $8.8 million—$235,000 more than the year before. Donald C. Cozzetti, administrative assistant to the Most Reverend Francis J. Green, bishop of the diocese, explained: "We make available each year approximately $1.2 million in loans to parishes and institutions, and we pay about the same amount to our total indebtedness." Sixty-six percent of the diocese's fund is spent on some form of service to the people, 27 percent is funneled into the debt service, and 7 percent is spent on administration. Also included in the Tucson statement was a "State of Souls" report. Serving as a kind of census, it tallied 75,788 families, 311 priests, 663 sisters and thirteen brothers in the nine-county diocese, which serves a geographical area of more than 52,000 square miles.

During 1970 the Wilmington, Delaware, Diocese published its first financial statement of operation and showed a balance of $24,846 after disbursements. For 1969 the total revenue reached a figure of $2,322,938, whereas the expenses were put at $2,298,092. The report cited the following revenues: parish contributions, $230,000; diocesan collection for special mission and other causes, $231,000; designated trust income, $50,000; departmental income, $707,000. What the report described as nonrecurring sources were the $809,000 from the diocesan development fund and $234,000 from bequest appropriations. The Wilmington statement showed that more than $200,000 of the revenue went to mission work, almost $88,000 to international causes, $33,000 to Catholic University and to Indian-Negro work on the national level, and $77,000 for local mission work and causes. Major disbursements were given to the diocese's education department, which received $126,211. Another large sum, $220,957, went to the Catholic Press of Wilmington, and $85,337 went for seminary education. If the diocese revenues remained at current levels, the report noted, the anticipated budget deficit for the next year would exceed $1.5 million.

For the fiscal year 1968–1969, the Archdiocese of Portland, Oregon, went into the hole $403,000, according to its report on the money spent by the chancery office—which did not include the finances of parishes, schools, religious orders or diocesan organizations. Archbishop Robert J. Dwyer's report said that aside from interest, which yielded $545,800, the biggest item of income was assessments on parishes, $476,000. His statement also listed income of $129,000 from bequests and gifts, $221,000 on the archdiocesan insurance program, $86,-000 in payments received on notes and contracts, $84,000 from special collections and $39,000 in grants from national organizations. A subsidy of $334,000 went to high schools, and another $230,000 went for the archdiocesan insurance program. To operate the chancery office cost $222,000. Interest on bank loans and notes was $592,000.

The Diocese of Winona, Minnesota, stated that its total assets in February 1970 were $10.6 million, its liabilities $2.4 million (no data on income and expenses were included). The Galveston-Houston Diocese in Texas reported total income of $14.7 million and total expenses of $13.3 million for the 1969 year.

At the end of December 1970 the Chicago Archdiocese, which had always held a hard line on divulging any information about its financial assets, unexpectedly made a public disclosure of its holdings and earnings. For the fiscal year that ended on June 30, the archdiocese reported its total assets at $85.5 million. It listed real-estate holdings ("exclusive of parish plants") at $6.5 million; primarily this consisted of 922 acres of vacant property spread throughout Cook and Lake Counties which had been acquired for future parish sites. The chancery reported that the market value of its investments in government and corporate securities came to $29.5 million. During the fiscal year the archdiocese had to sell $917,000 worth of its securities to meet operating expenses. Received from parish collections during the report period were approximately $53 million, of which about $50 million stayed in the parishes. John Cardinal Cody also stated that there were 456 churches, 420 elementary schools, eighty high schools, four seminaries, forty-eight cemeteries, and various other parish houses and health and welfare institutions.

In the first statement ever issued on the use of its funds, the New York Archdiocese showed that it operated at a deficit of more than $1.2 million during 1968. Income was listed as $14,263,000, which included gifts and bequests that totaled over $5.4 million. Terence Cardinal Cooke's fiscal statement showed $3,775,000 collected in Catholic Charities drives, $3,019,000 contributed by the parishes of the archdiocese, $4,405,000 from tuitions, and $3,064,000 from marketable investments, from royalties and from interest in notes receivable. The expenditures for New York came to over $20.9 million, of which health and welfare ($7.3 million), education ($11.6 million) and spiritual pastoral service ($2 million) comprised the lion's share. The chief reason for the $1.2-million deficit, the report stated, was the rising cost of education, especially in the twelve high schools operated by the archdiocese. The schools had an operating loss of $2.1 million; a sum of $1.3 million of archdiocesan funds was used to meet this loss. The report, which covered ten counties of the archdiocese (New York, Bronx, Richmond, Westchester, Putnam, Rockland, Orange, Sullivan, Ulster and Dutchess), did not include expenses accumulated by religious orders or the budgets of individual parishes and parochial elementary schools.*

In August 1968 the treasurer of the Cincinnati, Ohio, Archdiocese published some figures in *The Catholic Telegraph* which showed that the total amount of money expended in

* While this book was at the printer, the New York Archdiocese issued (in April 1972), with the assistance of a leading accounting firm, a report declaring its net worth to be $643 million. Nearly nine-tenths of the archdiocesan assets—$563 million—comprised "single purpose" land and properties suitable only for religious endeavor, the report stated. The remaining net assets were put at $51 million in cash, while other liquid assets and an endowment fund were valued at $29 million—this last figure included a securities portfolio approximating $13 million. Expenditures for the year ending August 31, 1971, came to a total of $127.5 million, according to the chancery, while income for the same period reached $125.9 million, leaving a deficit of $1.6 million.

the archdiocese came to $845,849. The sum received from eight special collections taken up each year in the parishes reached a figure of $1,578,000. Of this amount 53 percent was sent outside the archdiocese for eighteen different activities, while 47 percent was expended within the archdiocese.

The Diocese of La Crosse, Wisconsin, in a report covering the year which ended December 31, 1968, declared an income of $10,490,405 and expenses of approximately $8.5 million; the excess was over $2 million. The diocese said that most of its income came from the contributions of parishioners and the societies, which accounted for a total of $9.7 million. From property sales it realized $60,540, and from interest and dividends $45,974. A sum of over $665,000 was recorded from bequests and other similar contributions. On the debit side of the ledger, $6.7 million went for operations, another $1.3 million was absorbed into appropriations for agencies, and a total of $435,958 was used for interest payments. The La Crosse Diocese reported total assets of $87.8 million. Its properties, plants and equipment were valued at $84.9 million, and its cash on hand, representing the combined funds of the chancery and the parishes and missions, at $1.2 million. Under liabilities the diocese listed $7.5 million as its debt for external notes and mortgages. Total liabilities reached $9.2 million.

Although in the past the Archdiocese of St. Louis had published financial statements of various operations, it was not until January 1970 that the Archbishop, John Joseph Cardinal Carberry, presented for the first time a report on all phases of the archdiocese's operation simultaneously. Cardinal Carberry pointed out in a statement that as of the end of June 1969 the archdiocese owed a balance of $7.6 million on a $15-million loan negotiated several years previously for the construction of high schools. He also called attention to the large amount of money which the archdiocese borrowed from parishes and institutions, under payable notes amounting to over $25 million, and to the amount of funds which have been lent to parishes and institutions under receivable notes adding up to more than $19 million. As with similar reports from other parts of the country, the St. Louis Archdiocese is concerned with operating deficits and the erosion of reserves and capital assets to meet them.

Cardinal Carberry's financial report is divided into several parts and covers the many offices that comprise his archdiocese. But because there are a number of different year-end closings and since the 249 parishes make separate reports that are not included in the archdiocese figures, the financial statement still does not give a full picture, especially since the Catholic hospitals and educational facilities in the archdiocese, which are owned and operated by various religious orders, are not included. Nevertheless, the figures do give an idea of the Church's financial situation in St. Louis. For instance, the treasurer's office listed a revenue of nearly $3.3 million and expenses of over $4.3 million, leaving a deficit of $1,095,417. An excess of expenses over revenue for the seminaries ($229,-460) resulted from an income of $837,857 and an outlay of $1,067,317. In 1968 an area of operation known as the Archdiocesan Rural Life and Home Missions Conference and Tithing-for-the-Poor Plan listed its revenue as $304,635 and its expenses as $294,600, showing an excess of $10,035. The cemeteries showed a net income amounting to $225,653. On the other hand, the Catholic School Office listed an income of $204,797 and an outlay of $221,768, making a deficit of $16,971. The Catholic High School Association, however, showed a revenue figure of nearly $6.7 million and an expense summation of better than $5.4 million; this left an excess of more than $1.2 million, which was used to reduce the payable mortgage notes. The St. Louis Catholic school system had a total enrollment of 93,000 students distributed in 196 elementary schools and forty-four high schools. Ranking as one of the ten major Catholic school organizations in North America, the St. Louis system employs some 3,800 teachers. The official archdiocesan newspaper, *The St. Louis Review,* which is the largest weekly paper in Missouri and the fifth-largest diocesan newspaper in the United States, showed a deficit of $4,305, though it took in $287,366 from circulation and $236,853 from advertising. The unaudited report's various figures, which some parishioners hope will be the precursor of a complete financial statement, showed that assets came to about $75 million.

Under some heavy pressures, the Chicago Archdiocese finally put out its first financial statement in 1971, listing its assets at $85.5 million. The report also declared nearly $30 million stocks and bonds, plus 992 acres of vacant land to which it put a worth of $5.3 million. The archdiocese's income was put at $36.5 million, while the total income of the 456 parishes, which have aggregate assets of nearly $1.2 billion, was put at $53 million. Cardinal Cody's office also included a statement that showed the archdiocese's percentage of the parish collections as coming to $11.2 million, but this statement, like the other data, is unaudited.

Pittsburgh, Pennsylvania, is the only city in the United States where a professional accounting house was used to prepare a statement of diocesan receipts and disbursements. Arthur Young & Company was called in by Bishop John J. Wright, but the organization made clear in a covering letter to Auxiliary Bishop Vincent M. Leonard that its engagement did not contemplate an examination in accordance with generally accepted auditing standards. Thus all of the figures cited were prepared from diocesan books without audit.

The financial report of the Pittsburgh Diocese for the fiscal year that ended April 30, 1969, showed a total income of $3,431,430, with expenditures of $3,228,151. Excess of receipts over disbursements, therefore, was $203,279. The report listed among income nearly $1.2 million from parish assessments, $197,295 from general donations, and $176,937 from investments. A special Christmas offering brought in $240,847, and the Peter's Pence collection accounted for $107,244. The diocese's heaviest expense was its education program, for which over $1 million was spent. Another large expense was the schedule of disbursements for benevolent work in a variety of areas that included Biafra, Korea, South America, Poland, Lithuania, and Indian and Negro Catholic missions. The diocese also spent $340,219 for "the improvement of the social community in which we live." Under grants to parishes, institutions, agencies and religious communities, the diocese spent $591,506, and for administrative costs of the chancery the figure was put at $479,276. One of the largest sums in this last category was the salary schedule for both clergy and laity, which amounted to $72,469. In making the report public, Bishop Leonard said that a central finance office was to be established to make it easier in the future to draw up a yearly diocesan statement using general auditing standards.

In 1969, in lieu of a year-end financial report, the Milwaukee, Wisconsin, Archdiocese took another tack. The decision to give Roman Catholics in the area an inside look at the financial realities came after the archdiocese's 1968 campaign had brought in a disappointing $1.8 million, over $200,000 less than the previous year's. Joseph A. Deglman, a veteran of 150 public appeals in forty years, felt very strongly that the era of fund-raising drives had come to an end and that "something new" was needed to do the job. He believed that the community had never really been informed and that the contributors and even the priests did not indeed know what the needs were. Accordingly, during the 1969 drive to raise $2.75 million for charities and archdiocesan development Archbishop William E. Cousins revealed that a working budget of $3.6 million had been adopted. About a quarter of a million dollars would be raised from the sale of church property, he said in a taped radio message. The remainder, $2.75 million, would have to come from contributions and other sources. Over the air Archbishop Cousins explained that $433,000 was needed for chancery office operations, $2.1 million for education, and $1 million for charities. As had been expected by Mr. Deglman, the drive was a success.

Unlike the New York Archdiocese, which does publish a financial report, the Brooklyn Diocese—comprising the boroughs of Brooklyn and Queens and two counties of Long Island—has preferred not to make any kind of annual statement of its profits and losses. But an inkling of the extent of its financial operation can be obtained through an examination of the costs and expenses of the area's Catholic Charities. In 1968 the latter spent a record $54 million, which was $9.3 million more than the previous year. The largest single expenditure was $31.2 million for the health and hospitals division. Childcare services, the next biggest item, cost $14.8 million to provide assistance to 6,209 persons. The amounts spent in other categories were $4.1 million for families and the aged, $2.1 million for the Catholic Youth Organization, $475,166 for the emotionally disturbed, $296,411 for the deaf and the retarded, $190,015 for the blind, $71,649 for the unemployed and $805,552 for community development. Another item in the Brooklyn Archdiocese's total financial picture is the $60-million Catholic Medical Center of Brooklyn and Queens, which will have an $8-million research center when completed. In a few years, under strong central management, the number of beds in the center will have expanded to 1,700.

However energetic some dioceses are in keeping their business matters to themselves, there are times when chinks appear in the stony silence. Catholic officers who engage in this kind of secrecy, despite the unwanted images it creates, sometimes slip up and inadvertently disclose information about what their property is worth. Something of this nature happened several years ago in the Diocese of Lafayette, Louisiana. The diocese, which had been carrying some 1,500 insurance policies to cover 200-odd church properties in its jurisdiction, consolidated them into four, thereby saving $50,000 a year in premiums. Apparently the diocese had not sought any publicity about the matter, but a magazine specializing in insurance news divulged the details. Among the properties covered were a two-hundred-year-old church (an art masterpiece built by an octoroon) and the grave of Emmeline Labiche, the "maid of seventeen summers" who was immortalized as Evangeline. Altogether, 208 property locations in 145 different parishes were involved in the $47.5-million insurance package.

In a diocesan development-fund report for 1969, the Diocese of Richmond, Virginia, declared a total income of $877,-105, in contrast to a $550,000 income the year before. Loans made to parishes in 1969 at 4 percent interest amounted to $250,000, whereas in the previous year the total came to $100,000. As expected, the major outlay of money went to education, with $151,167 going to major seminarians and $126,-000 to a minor seminary. In 1968 these same expenditures came, respectively, to $88,423 and $101,876. In 1969 $100,338 was spent for the acquisition of diocesan property, as opposed to $51,396 in 1968.

Taking a cue from their bigger brothers, a number of small parishes in the United States have issued financial statements. Just two will be reported here.

St. Clement's Church in Center Line, Michigan, put out a fiscal report for the period ended December 31, 1967. It showed total cash received as $562,328 and a bank balance of $20,652—with a total income of $582,980. The church's total disbursements for that year came to $563,010, while the operating expenses were $497,676. The report also showed that the balance due on the church's archdiocesan loan was $139,378, on which it had paid $60,000 during the year.

Another parish that has followed suit is the St. Charles Borromeo Church of Kettering, Ohio. In a two-year report covering 1966 and 1967 the parish listed its income as $176,911 for the first year and $183,528 for the second. Its equity for the two years was put at $690,673 and $746,834. These figures comprised its church-school building ($699,375) and school and church equipment, rectory and office equipment and rectories. The land was valued at $62,909. Reporting total operational expenses as $113,773 for 1966 and $117,314 for 1967, the parish declared an excess of income over operating costs—$63,138 (1966) and $66,214 (1967).

Few, if any, of the aforementioned diocese and parish financial statements include any accounting of the business enterprises owned by the Church. Complicating the matter even more is the fact that the Catholic orders, since they are independent of archdiocese control and regulation in money matters, are never included in these reports, even when monks, brothers, nuns or sisters in a given archdiocese are engaged in commercial activities that bring in substantial revenue for their order. To dig out information about the orders' business enterprises and commercial activities, which government tax officers in Washington refer to irreverently as "monk business," is well-nigh impossible. Most Catholic leaders do indeed subscribe to the thesis that silence is not only golden but also worth its weight in gold. On the other hand, a little publicity now and then is relished by the best of us. The operation of the Franciscan nuns in Canton, Ohio, is a case in point.

When Mother Superior Mary Angelica of the Sisters of Sancta Clara Monastery in Canton, Ohio, was seeking a way to raise funds to build another convent, someone proposed that the order raise and sell red worms to local fishermen. Appalled at the thought of worms squirming all over her convent, Mother Angelica hit upon another idea—why not make artificial fishing lures and sell them instead? The Franciscan nuns, guided by a sister who had once been a pretty good angler, set about making attractive dry and wet flies for fly-fishing. Inevitably, the Cleveland *Plain Dealer* heard about it and gave it a big story in its sport pages. The result was astounding. Newspapers throughout the country picked up the item, and before long several mass-circulation magazines did features on the "fishing-lure nuns." Orders began pouring in from all over the United States and even from abroad. That was in 1961. Today the fishing-lure business has been shifted to the new convent in Birmingham, Alabama, which was built with the profits from the business several years ago. Orders come in at the rate of nearly $2,000 a month, including regular purchases from customers like Ted Williams, the former outfielder for the Boston Red Sox. To keep up with the demand, the nuns put in an eight-hour workday, each making as many as a hundred lures an hour. The product is sold under the brand name of St. Peter's Fishing Lures, named after the first Pope, who was himself a fisherman.

Other convents may not have received as much publicity as the cloistered nuns of Canton and Birmingham, but they are quietly running profitable businesses of their own. For instance, the Trappistine nuns of Wrentham, Massachusetts, manufacture a variety of expensive candies which are sold in candy shops throughout the nation. The Dominican Sisters of Mission San José of California operate an extensive mail-order business which specializes in fruitcakes. The sales are made from two convents in Los Angeles, one in Anaheim, and one at San Gabriel. Nuns of the St. Boniface Parish in Detroit run a parking lot next to the stadium of the Detroit Tigers baseball team and the Detroit Lions football team. In their advertising signs the nuns claim, "We Never Scrape Fenders!" At Jamaica Plain, not far from Boston, the Daughters of St. Paul own a profitable printing plant which puts out hundreds of thousands of books each year. In West Palm Beach, Florida, the Carmelite Sisters operate the 250-room Pennsylvania Hotel, which they purchased in 1964 for $800,000. On twenty-one acres of a ninety-acre site owned by the Franciscan Sisters of Wheaton, Illinois, an $8-million housing project is being built with federal funds. Sister Virginia Mary, provincial director, has made it known that her order will not use its tax-exempt status and will pay real-estate taxes on the building. A summer camp for girls in the Rocky Mountains is operated near Evergreen, Colorado, by St. Rita's Court of the Catholic Daughters of America.

Equally as active in the commercial world are the men's Catholic orders. Take the Trappist monks, for example. Kentucky farmers in general do not arise at two-fifteen in the morning to begin work, but the 250 men of the Abbey of Gethsemani at Trappist, Kentucky, get up at that hour every day, many of them to tend their cows and pigs and perform other farming chores. The monks and brothers in this farming community cultivate eight hundred acres of land (half of which is irrigated by fourteen monk-made lakes) and take care of 1,200 acres of woodland. On their farm they produce corn, cereal grains, sorghum, alfalfa, clover, orchard grass and bluegrass. Most of these crops are used to feed their herd of about a hundred registered Holstein cows. The milk of the Holstein is especially good for making cheese, which is what the Trappist monks of Kentucky produce and sell. In a modern plant with tile walls and stainless-steel equipment, the monks make five varieties of cheeses, which are processed and stored in a series of cooling rooms designed to simulate conditions inside a cave. Placed on wooden racks where they are washed with a brine solution, the cheeses are turned over every other day, and after three months of curing they are sold on the open market. Much of the distribution is through mail orders. The cheeses, by the way, are made according to a secret Trappist formula which originated in a monastery in France and which is known by only one monk at Gethsemani.

A few years ago the monks began making fruitcakes, and these too have proved a popular item, especially at Christmas time, when mail orders are heavy. Other products produced at the Gethsemani farm include ham, sausages, bacon and a now famous dark whole-wheat bread. The monks also run a hay-pelleting operation which is based on many advanced techniques and is one of the best in the country. In addition, because they sow and fertilize their fields according to scientific soil tests, they are able to raise top-grade alfalfa on what farming experts would consider poor land. Apart from what they use for their own livestock, the monks sell about a thousand tons of alfalfa pellets each year at approximately $55 a ton to nearby Bluegrass horse farms and to turkey breeders.

The Kentucky monks, who spend almost as much time each day on meditation and prayer as they do on their farming operation, are not the only order in the United States engaged in producing a product which is sold on the commercial market. At Spencer, Massachusetts, the Trappist monks of St. Joseph's Abbey run a 2,300-acre farm and produce twenty-seven flavors of jelly, which is marketed in all of the fifty states and Canada. St. Benedict's Abbey in Aspen, Colorado, operates a 3,800-acre ranch with five hundred head of cattle, and its beef brings prime prices. The Benedictine Fathers of Collegeville, Minnesota, operate KSJN-FM, the most powerful FM radio station in the state. The men of the Abbey of Genesee, New York, have a modern automatic bakery in which they produce their popular Monk's Bread. They advertise the bread with a sketch of a friar whose cowled head is bent in thought, under which runs this salable copy: "Monk's Bread has a flavor you can't toast away. Even butter can't hide it. It has a goodness you don't find in most bread. It's a bread that wasn't meant to be sold. . . ."

Near Dubuque, Iowa, the Cistercian monks have a dairy and beef business on their two thousand acres of land. This order also operates an apple orchard, a bakery, an apiary, a large alfalfa dehydrating plant, a sawmill and a stone quarry. White Monk Foods are owned by the Cistercian Monastery of Okauchee, Wisconsin; Monastery Bread is made by the Trappist monks of Berryville, Virginia; and the oranges which come from St. Leo, Florida, are raised by the Benedictine Fathers there. At Ashland, Montana, the Capuchin priests of St. Joseph own a costume-jewelry business which has a large mail-order clientele and does close to a million dollars of business each year. The Marist Fathers in Hawaii operate a recording studio and plant where they make records of Hawaiian music, which sell well all over the islands, mostly to tourists, as well as on the mainland. The Carthusian Order of monks, using a secret formula of its own, manufacture and market a liqueur which it calls Chartreuse. Near Belleville, Illinois, the Oblate Fathers have a plush motel called Pilgrim's Inn, attached to which are a large restaurant and a gift shop. Nearby is a Catholic-owned retirement home called Apartment Community, atop which is the tower for radio station WMRY-FM, also run by the Oblate Fathers as a commercially profitable enterprise. In Minnesota St. John's Abbey receives a royalty on every loaf of "St. John's Bread" sold by baking companies in six states, and the abbey near St. Cloud owns a secret recipe for a pumpernickel-type bread called *Schwarzbrot* whose formula the Benedictine monks brought with them from Bavaria over a century ago. The Cistercian monastery near Paulding, Mississippi, operates a 320-acre farm on which a herd of registered Herefords grazes; Father Remigius Kozak herds cattle six days a week on horseback in cowboy gear and gives Mass in two different churches on Sundays. In western Colorado, at Snowmass, St. Benedict's Monastery owns 3,500 acres of land, of which 1,500 have been irrigated. The monks make a fine-quality hard candy and raise Hereford cattle; the revenue from these activities is applied to the mortgage on the property, the building program and operating expenses. In Canada, at Arnprior, Ontario, the brothers of the Oblate Novitiate of Mary Immaculate do a $25,000-a-year business raising and marketing pheasants for the dinner table. They retail the birds at thirteen dollars a pair, plucked, cleaned, quick-frozen and attractively packaged. Members of the order sell their entire production in Toronto, Montreal and Ottawa. The Novitiate of Los Gatos, California, after operating a 385-acre vineyard for over half a century, sold most of the land a few years ago for $5 million to a development firm, which is turning the prime acres into one-family homesites.

One Catholic group of men which is not interested in producing commodities to be put on the market is the Marianists of Ohio. This Franciscan order subscribes to the view that it is not interested in owning property, running companies or dealing in real estate. To finance its charitable work abroad, the Marianists, who own the University of Dayton, conduct a direct-mail fund-raising enterprise that nets them about $400,000 a year. Several types of appeals are sent through the mails at various times of the year to Roman Catholics. Around Easter, for instance, recipients might get an invitation to make "a spiritual bouquet," which would be accompanied by a card bearing a printed prayer and a self-addressed envelope. Though these mail requests bring in receipts that total nearly $1.6 million, with operating costs getting higher and higher each year, not to mention a payroll for a staff of some 50 laymen, the Marianists find themselves with expenses that run close to $1.2 million. Significantly, before the fiscal year is out, the some $400,000 that remains after expenditures is used on the order's budgeted mission program.

A favorite business activity of the Catholic Church is cemeteries, but these are nearly always run by the dioceses or the archdioceses rather than by the orders. Catholic cemeteries throughout the United States number close to a thousand and are a source of steady profit, even with the payment of real-estate taxes. In Chicago alone the archdiocese owns and operates twenty-four different burial grounds, from which, at year end, it shows substantial gain.

Generally speaking, the archdioceses do not engage in the operation of businesses *per se*. There are, however, a few exceptions. Several years ago, for instance, the Seattle Archdiocese purchased for over $1 million the New Washington Hotel, a structure with a colorful past, which had housed gold hunters back from Alaska and had been used as a stopping place by American Presidents from Theodore to Franklin D. Roosevelt. Staffed today by the Sisters of St. Joseph of Newark, the landmark hotel, now known as the Josephinum, is a fourteen-story residential hotel with 250 rooms housing senior citizens who pay monthly charges ranging from $50 to $300 (for the penthouse); the Josephinum requires no down payment and will, at an extra charge, serve breakfast and dinner to those occupants who wish it. The Catholic diocese of Austin, Texas, owns the Newton Asphalt Company, which occupies seven acres of land in an industrial-park area on the outskirts of Alexandria, Virginia. The New York Archdiocese had for many years a half interest in the sales royalties of Listerine, but sold it a few years ago for $25 million. And in Boston the archdiocese sold its ownership of station WIHS-TV for $2,276,513 in 1966. The Denver Archdiocese operates a summer camp in Colorado's cool mountains, Camp St. Malo near Allenspark.

American Catholic business also includes at least one notable instance of a seminary having commercial interests. This is the Pontifical College Josephinum at Worthington, Ohio. Of the 124 seminaries in the United States, only one is directly subject to the Holy See in Rome. Often called "the Pope's American Seminary," the Pontifical College Josephinum operates under a constitution signed by Ernest Cardinal Ruffini and approved by Pope Pius XI in 1938. Today Pope Paul VI supervises his seminary through the Apostolic Delegate in Washington. Some five hundred priests, working in nearly every state, are alumni of the Josephinum. The seminary does not derive any funds from the Holy See, but exists through the contributions of thousands of generous benefactors, whose gifts are invested in varying enterprises. Recently, for example, $2 million was put into building a motor hotel in nearby Columbus. With a staff of about a hundred employees, the Christopher Inn is a sixteen-level circular motel which has three decks for parking 150 cars, and 140 rooms for patrons. There are dining facilities for five hundred persons, meeting rooms, a landscaped terrace and a swimming pool. The motel's sidewalks and driving ramps can be heated so as to remain snow- and ice-free in winter. In addition to the Christopher Inn, the Josephinum owns a parking lot in downtown Columbus which used to be the site of an A & P food store; the city's old bus station at Town and Third Streets, now vacant; and the building which once housed Columbus' Montgomery Ward store and which is now leased, in part, to the U. S. Internal Revenue Service after having been refurbished for nearly $600,000. As for the historic downtown Neil House hotel building, contrary to some rumors, it was never owned by the Josephinum but by Archbishop V. J. Sheil of the Chicago Archdiocese, who sold it to four Akron businessmen for a reported $5 million.

Some Catholic businesses, unlike the Josephinum operations, are rather difficult to pin down as to direct ownership. Such is the case with several insurance companies in Omaha, Nebraska. A number of companies in that insurance town enjoy a quasi-relationship with the Roman Catholic Church, but just how this relationship is structured has never been made clear. The companies in question are the Catholic Relief Insurance Company, the Catholic Workman Life Insurance Association, the Catholic Mutual Relief Society, and the Mutual Protective Insurance Company. The last-named organization advertises itself as "the Catholic's Company." Similarly, the Catholic Association of Foresters, which has offices in Fort Lauderdale, Florida, and Hamden, Connecticut, tells clients it is "chartered by law to serve Catholics only." To date it has paid out more than $65 million in benefits to its members.

While Catholic business activities mentioned here have placed vast financial resources at clerical fingertips, one of the most lucrative sources of revenue for the Church is the government. A study made in Denver, Colorado, to determine the breakdown of a $14.5-million grant to sectarian institutions disclosed that over 90 percent was allocated to the Catholic Church, though only about one third of the religious community in that city adhered to the Catholic religion.

Government subsidies to churches—frequently viewed as a violation of the First Amendment, as well as of many explicit state-constitution provisions—are involved in such a diversity of programs, many of them overlapping and interlocking and many hidden in such a confusing array of overt and covert fronts, that one Congressional committee several years ago gave up trying to tabulate all of them in one single volume. Of some 250 federal aid-to-education programs, let us cite just one that comes to attention under the title of Urban Redevelopment, a federal program carried out in cooperation with municipal governments. Since clergymen of all faiths sit on local Urban Renewal boards, there is naturally a concerted effort on each man's part to get as much as he can for his own denomination or school. Five Roman Catholic universities—Duquesne University of Pittsburgh, Fordham University of New York, King's College in Pennsylvania, Marquette University of Milwaukee and St. Louis University in Missouri—have been, among other schools, the recipients of Urban Redevelopment largesse. For instance, Duquesne University acquired for $1 million a parcel of land which had cost the government some $11 million; Duquesne then constructed buildings on the site with government loans and other subsidies.

Ultimately, some church officials get preferential treatment. In the administration of the Hill-Burton Act,* for example, favoritism is quite visible. More than $300 million in government funds have gone into the building of Catholic hospitals in the United States since 1947, whereas the Protestant and Jewish religions have cumulatively received some $170 million. From 1947 to 1958 the Catholic Church averaged the sum of $14 million a year from this progam, but this annual figure has gradually increased since 1961 and is now $30.5 million.

Since 1946 the Department of Health, Education and Welfare has been giving to sectarian groups parcels of federal surplus lands and buildings, properties ranging from old barracks and vacant lots to complete modern hospitals with surrounding grounds. In theory, H.E.W. is obliged to distribute these properties to sectarian groups representing all religions, at discounts averaging 95 percent of their "fair value." This fuzzy designation represents a tiny part of the property's real value or original cost.

Before the administration of President John F. Kennedy—

* Passed originally in 1946, the Hill-Burton Act (which has been extended several times since) provides construction funds for private and sectarian hospitals.

that is, between 1946 and the middle part of 1961—Catholic organizations were the recipients of about 24 percent of this property, or approximately the same proportion as that of American Catholics to the total population of the United States. Following the arrival of the New Frontier, the Catholic share skyrocketed to nearly 94 percent of the total church giveaways. Although President Kennedy himself believed separation of church and state to be fundamental to the American heritage and was opposed to the federal government's extending support to sustain any church or its schools, a number of his appointees showed favoritism to the Catholics. There is no record to show whether the President had any awareness of this favoritism. During the first two fiscal years of the New Frontier, the Catholic Church acquired properties worth $8.7 million—$1.5 million more than it had acquired from 1946 to mid-1961. The same source that divulged these figures—H.E.W.'s "Transfers of Real Properties to Denominationally Sponsored Organizations for Health and Welfare"—also revealed that during the 1962–63 fiscal year the Catholic Church received properties valued at $7.6 million, while all other American religious groups combined were given an unimpressive $15,000.

No one as yet has been able to add up precisely how much money federal agencies have given churches in the way of grants. One careful researcher, Adele Porter, former managing editor of *Church and State* magazine, has estimated that the figure comes to better than $5.5 billion, of which nearly three quarters goes to Catholic organizations. Moreover, at least another billion dollars from state and city treasuries is granted each year to churches of all denominations. Miss Porter observes that had such sectarian benefits been curtailed, the unpopular surtax that Washington imposed in 1968 would not have been needed.

Most of these grants are never publicized unless there is a

"newsworthy" event connected with it. For instance, when R. Sargent Shriver, then head of the Office of Economic Opportunity (which disburses about $90 million a year to antipoverty programs run by churches), spoke at the Diamond Jubilee Banquet of the Sisters of the Blessed Sacrament and presented a government check for $7 million to the Natchez-Hattiesburg Diocese, he was given celebrity treatment by the local press. If it had not been for the presence of Mr. Shriver, chances are the $7-million handout would have gone completely unnoticed.

5

TAXES ARE A FOUR-LETTER WORD

When more of the people's sustenance is exacted through the form of taxation than is necessary to meet the just obligations of government . . . such exaction becomes ruthless extortion and a violation of the fundamental principles of a free government.—GROVER CLEVELAND

HUBERT SCHIEFELBEIN was born in Topeka, Kansas, of German parentage in 1911. Some twenty years later, when his efforts to get a football scholarship to the University of Southern California failed, he found work in the spice department of a coffee company. Later he won a promotion to the company's mustard section and in time Hubert Schiefelbein became head of the department. He quit the company some years later, bought a gasoline station and eventually acquired a second one. Successful but unhappy, the Kansan decided to leave the business world and apply for admission to the Christian Brothers, a teaching order of the Roman Catholic Church. Madness? Not quite.

Today Hubert Schiefelbein is a successful businessman once again. As Brother Urban Gregory, F.S.C., he is the head of a multimillion-dollar winery and distillery which provide considerable income for his order's extensive teaching operations. The Christian Brothers began their winemaking operations humbly in 1879, making small quantities of table wine, and gradually word of its excellence spread. As was to be expected, occasionally someone would ask to buy some. And so the Christian Brothers found themselves, on a very modest scale, in the wine business.

In 1932 the Brothers acquired a large parcel of land and some new mission-style buildings in the western foothills of the Napa Valley. On the property was an old stone winery and approximately two hundred acres of grapes grown from German and French cuttings that had been brought to the United States by the former owner. Over the years the wines that the Christian Brothers made from these grapes earned a reputation for fine quality, and the Brothers' business prospered. The Christian Brothers winery is now one of the largest wine producers in the United States and profits from the operation are helping to carry on the order's expanding educational work and to support thirteen institutions of learning in California and Oregon.

There have, however, been occasional storms over the sunny Napa Valley vineyards. An embittered competitor pointed out that the Christian Brothers, who had become the largest manufacturers of commercial brandy in America, were not paying any tax on their profits. And at a hearing before a House Subcommittee on Internal Revenue Taxation in 1956, author Paul Blanshard, a special counsel representing Americans United of Washington, D.C., exhibited two bottles of Christian Brothers brandy and wine and asked if such production was really church business. "To bring such activity under a clerical tax exemption," Mr. Blanshard said, "is to make a mockery of the whole concept of the function of religious institutions in our society."

Concerned over the negative publicity from the hearings,

the Christian Brothers began paying taxes in 1957. After they had paid $490,000, however, they quietly filed suit to get the money back on the grounds that they had been illegally taxed. Because of intense public interest, the federal government countersued for all back taxes. The case, Number 7499 in the United States District Court for the Northern District of California, revealed what sort of profits the Christian Brothers winery was making. For instance, for the years 1952, 1953 and 1956, net profits came to $3,250,000. Since these figures excluded the 1957–60 period, during which the Brothers had expanded their operation considerably, California winemakers speculated that the total net profits were well beyond $7 million.

Arguing that the order had chapel services at its winery and that all its property was "subject to the control of the Pope," the Christian Brothers maintained it was exempt as a church. Federal Judge Sherrill Halbert, in a decision handed down in Sacramento in July 1961, did not agree. Rather than appeal the judgment, possibly as a result of instructions from higher-ups who feared that the case might draw attention to other church business enterprises, the Christian Brothers accepted a settlement. The organization agreed to pay the federal government $631,668 in additional taxes, plus $281,595 in interest for the protested years 1952, 1953 and 1956, and $1,880,530 in taxes for 1954, 1955 and 1957, plus $683,595 interest. Inasmuch as the Christian Brothers did not recover income taxes already paid, the total amount the winery had to give Uncle Sam came to well over $3.5 million. Today the Christian Brothers winery meets all its state and federal tax commitments like any other business.

Contrast the case of the Christian Brothers with that of "the world's richest nun," Katharine Drexel of Philadelphia. When Anthony J. Drexel, a partner of J. P. Morgan, died in 1893, he left his daughter Katharine $15 million and an income estimated at $1,000 a day. Four years later, at the age of twenty-nine, Katharine joined a religious order and took the vow of poverty, after which she could not touch a penny of her inheritance. In 1921 Congress enacted a complex law to enable Katharine, now a mother superior, to give the income from her inherited millions to charity, tax free. Several years later Mother Katharine's charitable giving was further eased by Congressional approval of another complex formula, a formula that became known in money circles as the "Philadelphia Nun tax loophole." To generations of tax lawyers since then, that loophole has been the means by which supremely wealthy lay individuals, corporations and religious organizations can avoid paying taxes on billions of dollars.

At the Senate Finance Committee hearings on tax reform several years ago, statistics were brought in to show that churches and related organizations enjoy an income cash flow of about $21 billion. Of this, some $9 billion comes from voluntary contributions, about $6.5 billion from business operations, investment income, foundation grants and tax-exempt bequests, and another $5.5 billion from government grants and subsidies to churches. If the business income of churches were taxed and if the capital appreciation of gifts and bequests were subjected to capital-gains taxation, the Senators were told, the United States Treasury would be richer by $5 billion. One witness put the value of church-held properties and investments as high as $102 billion and cited a 26 percent increase over a four-year period.

Careful estimates indicate that better than half this wealth is owned by the Roman Catholic Church. But it is the contention of many Catholic officials that the beneficent works of their Church in the community at large justify tax exemptions. Church income, they maintain, is financing Catholic-run colleges and schools, hospitals, overseas missions and welfare agencies. In recent years the Catholic Church has also been pouring considerable aid into black neighborhoods. Public-opinion polls indicate that there is widespread support for continuing tax-exempt status of land and buildings used by the Catholic Church for worship.

When, however, in 1968 the Columbia Broadcasting System conducted a poll and asked, "Do you think that religious institutions should pay taxes on the income they get from business or commercial operations which have nothing to do with religious activities?" the response showed that 84 percent of the general public favored taxation of such unrelated income, as did 93 percent of the clergy.

The blame for raising the question of church tax exemption is often assigned to Madalyn Murray O'Hair, who, after winning her suit for banning prayers in the public schools, instituted legal proceedings which questioned the exemption of church property from taxation. Indeed, Mrs. O'Hair made the issue a very live one, but she was not by any means the first to talk about the matter publicly. The issue and the agitation are not new. James Madison raised the question and spoke ominously of "encroachment by Ecclesiastical Bodies" when he opened a discussion on a proposal in Kentucky to exempt churches from taxes. Early in the nineteenth century, many of the states engaged in debates on the issue and enacted laws when the question of legality was raised. Ever since, controversy has raged around the issue of the separation of church and state.

Today the rumblings come mostly from the suburbs. As the Catholic Church followed its adherents from the central city to the outlying areas, putting up new church buildings as it went (in 1970 nearly $1 billion was spent on these structures), more and more parcels of land have been removed from the tax rolls. Real-estate taxation provides most of the revenue for new communities, and the property owners who must pay the taxes are sensitive to a church's buying up land

and removing it from the list of eligible taxpaying properties. Several years ago a Catholic bishop, hoping to establish a new diocese in an Eastern community, gobbled up so much territory that a delegation of the most prestigious Catholics in the area visited him and lodged a passionate plea for him to cease acquiring any more lots there.

While none of the churches—Catholic, Protestant or Jewish—is the largest owner of exempt property (government being the holder of this distinction), it is a fact that whenever an additional piece of church property receives an exempt classification (throwing an increased burden on the remaining realty), people will react critically to the exempt property. Often what is visible to everyone, especially if the local newspaper prints a story on the subject, is that a church is getting away with not paying taxes on a choice lot. This same church might well have several other lots lying around unused, and when and if that church sells a piece of real estate that has gone up in value, the squawking is often loud. Inasmuch as some Catholic churches have invested in land with a profit-making intent, knowing full well no taxes would have to be paid on the land while its value appreciated, the public is likely to make its negative views known. A dictum of American life is that anyone who pays taxes disapproves of anyone who does not.

The amount of church-owned property in the nation is so vast and complex that few definitive estimates have been made of its total value. Based on inspections of tax records, assessment lists and land studies, the estimated total value of real estate owned today by the various religious organizations in the nation is somewhere between $79.5 billion and $100 billion. Of this, approximately $44.5 billion belongs to the Catholic Church, whose holdings apparently rival those of the first five American corporations (Standard Oil of New Jersey, $12 billion; General Motors, $10.8 billion; Ford Motor, $5.9 billion;

United States Steel, $5.1 billion; and Socony Mobil Oil, $4.7 billion), which total $38.5 billion. In New York City religious institutions own property that is worth over $690 million. If taxed, this property would bring in more than $35 million in revenue each fiscal year. Several years ago, New York's Temporary Commission on City Finances urged a reevalution of the city's exemption policies, noting that "the gap between New York's mounting costs of operation and its income from real estate taxes is widened by the withdrawal of more and more property from the tax rolls." Alarmed by the rapid growth of exemptions, the commission urged that such overly generous immunities be cut back.

It should also be noted in passing that the Vatican pays no taxes on its commercial interests in the Untied States. The exemption can be based either on its being a church or on its being a foreign government. Section 892 of the Internal Revenue Code states that the "income from foreign governments . . . received from investments in the United States . . . shall not be included in gross income and shall be exempt from taxation. . . ." Since the Bureau of Internal Revenue has classified the Vatican as a foreign government, the Vatican is exempt from taxation.

But of all the forms of tax benefit enjoyed by the Catholic Church in the United States, none is more controversial than the exemption from taxes on unrelated business income. Universities are now required to pay taxes on businesses they own that are not directly related to education, but church lobbies have shown themselves more effective than educational blocs. For instance, after it became known that New York University owned the Mueller Spaghetti Company and was not paying taxes on the profits from the sale of spaghetti and noodles, Congress passed a bill whereby exemption income was limited to organizational enterprises directly related to the purpose of the cited organization; at the last minute, however, an amendment was attached, continuing the exemptions on the churches' unrelated business activities. Thus the tax ax fell on the schools but not on the churches or on church-related schools.

It is not always easy to draw the line between a related and an unrelated business. A government tax officer has defined the related business this way: "If it is an integral part of its church organization, essential to the effective pursuit of its religious programs and not a device for financial profit from an outside enterprise, it is related." Even so, the distinction is sometimes difficult to make. Take, for example, the case of St. Joseph's Catholic Church, in Meppen, Illinois, and its turtle soup. The church bases its operating budget largely on the income from the sale of this soup at an annual picnic; the soup is prepared and sold by the church's three hundred members, who donate their services. The annual enterprise, which was begun in 1920, now brings in some $12,500 each year, and the question arose, is it a tax-exempt "related business" or a taxable "unrelated business"? The local and state tax authorities of Illinois have not found it to be unrelated, or taxable, because the income derives "from a business which is regularly carried on by the organization" and which is "substantially related to the organization's exempt purpose."

Secular leaders, and many church leaders (most of them Protestant), charge that such exemptions constitute tax favoritism by Congress and are discriminatory against commercial businesses in the same field. The critics claim that the churches should not become involved in business for profit, and that if they do go into business, they should pay the tax collector. Hard-pressed church leaders disagree and say that if the church is to tend to the spiritual and temporal needs of the community, it must deal in business enterprises unrelated to church worship. They point out that if hospitals, orphan asylums and other welfare institutions were not maintained by the churches (often with income from tax-exempt enterprises), the state would have to provide these services, with a resulting increase in rates for the taxpayer. The church, it is held, is therefore relieving the state of additional financial obligations.

With the costs of local government continuing to soar, there have been some tax crackdowns on many properties owned by or otherwise affiliated with churches. But this does not mean that these exemptions are a thing of the past. Not at all. In fact, the tax shelter protecting religious properties is still reasonably watertight.

In 1969, Governor Ronald Reagan of California signed into law a bill stipulating that the state's corporation tax be applied to unrelated businesses directly operated by religious organizations. In arguing for passage of the bill, its sponsor, Democratic State Senator Anthony C. Beilenson, pointed out that California was one of the few jurisdictions that had eliminated churches' exemption with regard to property taxes. He said:

> Churches must pay taxes on all property they own, except for the church structure itself. We are very strict in this. Even the residence of the clergy and parts of the church structure which are used for non-religious purposes are taxed. Thus we find ourselves in the position of requiring that the church pay property taxes on its business property because the business is unrelated to the religious activity, yet we do not tax the income from this very same business. This exemption is also inequitable because these businesses accept the benefits of our society, but we do not require that they pay for these same services. These businesses use our courts to enforce their contracts, and their plants are protected by our police and firemen, but they do not share the burden of these costs. Rather, this burden is placed on other taxpayers. A second reason is that other businesses are at a distinct disadvantage when they must compete against a church-

owned commercial enterprise. Taxes are a cost of production and an important overhead factor. Thus, a church-owned business, not subject to the same taxes, has a major competitive advantage over its commercial rivals.

California's new law, which became effective in January 1970, requires all churches in the state to list types and sources of income. The amount of such income need not be reported, however, unless it derives from an unrelated business. Cemeteries, publications, old-age homes and other activities directly associated with church functioning remain tax-free.

The United States Congress made an attempt at tax-reform legislation in 1969. By 394 to 30 the House of Representatives voted in favor of a provision to abolish tax exemptions on church income derived from business unrelated to religion. In an unprecedented action, both the General Board of the National Council of Churches and the U. S. Roman Catholic hierarchy joined in asking the House Ways and Means Committee to tax income from unrelated church business.

Shortly before House passage of the bill, Father Robert J. Henle, S.J., president of Georgetown University in Washington, D.C., warned the Ways and Means Committee of dangers in certain other proposed tax reforms. The educator asserted that some of the bill's provisions concerning individual gifts of appreciated property would either deprive the public of certain services from religious institutions or transfer them completely to public budgets. Existing tax advantages were "not loopholes," he said, but strategic and enlightened legislative provisions to "help shift some of the burdens of public service to the private sector and to promote independent public service at minimal cost to the taxpayer." He said that the "immediate increase in revenue would ultimately be dearly bought."

In one of the recent key cases bearing directly on whether churches should lose their tax exemptions, Frederick Walz of the Bronx in New York City went all the way to the United States Supreme Court. His goal was to change the tax structure in every state in the union.

Mr. Walz had purchased a weed-filled plot of worthless land, twenty-two by twenty-nine feet, near a junkyard in an old neighborhood in Staten Island. Valued at a mere one hundred dollars, the land was assessed $5.24 a year in real-estate taxes. Mr. Walz sued the New York City Tax Commission for violating his constitutional rights, contending that the $5.24 tax represented a violation of the First Amendment. Though he was not a member of any religious organization, he maintained, New York State laws exempting church property from taxation made his own tax higher and forced him indirectly and involuntarily to support churches. The Walz suit contested the tax exemption of religious organizations but not that of their schools, hospitals or other charitable institutions. Three New York State trial and appeals courts dismissed the case, but Mr. Walz, himself a nonpracticing counselor at law, kept filing written appeals. The New York State Supreme Court ruled that "such exemptions are granted in pursuance of long-standing policy of this state, under a statute that is presumably Constitutional."

Persisting, Mr. Walz eventually succeeded in getting the U. S. Supreme Court to hear the case and rule on the constitutionality of church tax exemption. He himself did not appear before the Supreme Court; his case was argued by Edward J. Ennis, chairman of the American Civil Liberties Union. Mr. Ennis took the position that the first ten words of the First Amendment, "Congress shall make no law respecting an establishment of religion," were sufficiently vague to give rise to the possibility that tax exemption of church property was tantamount to supporting religious institutions. He argued further that the two-hundred-year-old precedent of religious-property-tax exemption could be attributed to the gradual accumulation of political power on the part of religious organizations, and that discontinuance of that exemption would promote the neutrality required by the doctrine of separation of church and state. He pointed out that the "land used by a newspaper in printing a paper is just as important to the freedom of the press as a church used in freedom of religion."

Defending the lower-court decisions was J. Lee Rankin, corporation counsel for New York City. He argued that assessment of church property at market value would be burdensome for most churches, especially those, like St. Patrick's Cathedral, that were located in high-rent areas. He also took issue with the argument that tax exemption was the same as aid; he called it "neutral," neither aid nor penalty. Mr. Rankin said that discontinuing tax exemption would seriously inhibit the ability of the religious institutions to provide society with public services such as hospitals for the care of the sick and the elderly and the numerous parochial schools maintained throughout the country. He told the Supreme Court that the churches' tax-exempt status was now so deeply ingrained that its abolition would upset the neutrality between church and state and infringe on churchmen's free exercise of their religion. Churches, he said, had proceeded for two hundred years on the assumption that they would not have to pay taxes, and if that were changed some congregations might have to abandon their chapels.

In May 1970 the Supreme Court announced a seven–one decision to uphold state laws exempting from taxation property used solely for religious purposes. The high court ruled that such laws do not violate the First Amendment. Chief Justice Warren E. Burger said that such tax exemptions have not given the "remotest sign of leading to an established church or religion, and on the contrary it has operated affirmatively to help guarantee the free exercise of all forms of religious beliefs. The grant of tax exemption is not sponsorship, since the government does not transfer part of its revenue to churches but simply abstains from demanding that the church support the state." He emphasized that New York was simply sparing the exercise of religion from the burden of property taxation levied on private profit institutions. The opinion left many questions unanswered, one of them whether a state may tax religiously used properties if it so decides.

Shortly before the Supreme Court's decision, the state of New Jersey set up a commission to study laws that exempted real property held by religious, educational, charitable and philanthropic organizations and cemeteries from taxation. Headed by Assemblyman Chester Apy of Monmouth County, the commission took more than a year to review the pros and cons of the issue. In January 1970, it issued a seventy-page report. The commission could not recommend any appreciable change in the exemptions provided by the state for property used exclusively for religious, educational, charitable or cemetery purposes. The Apy Commission pointed out that there are some 143 hospitals in New Jersey, of which one hundred are voluntary, nonprofit hospitals, forty are government hospitals and three are private, profit-making hospitals, and that most of the municipalities in the state do not have a hospital. "Thus . . . residents must depend upon the hospital in some neighboring community for hospital services. The same situation holds true for colleges and universities, probably for many churches, and for many other exempt properties," the report stated.

Although the commission concluded that most of the present exemptions would have to remain unchanged, it did not feel that the current "inequitable distribution of exempt property" and the "consequent variable burdens of such exemptions on the local taxpayers" should continue. In view of the inequity inherent in New Jersey's situation, the Apy Commission recommended that the burden of exemption from real-property taxes be equalized among the taxing districts in each county, and it worked out this formula:

Each of the municipalities in a given county would compute the cost (that is, the loss of revenue) to itself through statutory exemption of property from regular taxation, by calculating the amount of the tax that would be paid on such property (at the currently established rate for taxable property) if it were not exempt. This amount would be measured against the total amount payable by the nonexempt real property in the municipality in terms of percentage. Similar computations would be made in relation to the amounts of tax payable and of revenue lost through statutory exemption, for the entire county. Each municipality then would receive an increase or decrease in its share of county taxes in accordance with the degree to which its exemption percentage exceeded or fell short of the county percentage.

Allowing that this was not a precise formula for correcting the imbalance in the distribution of exempt property, the Apy Commission felt that it established a method for determining what municipalities lose by having exempt properties within their borders—that is, the ability to derive from the exempt acres the same amount of taxes that they derive from taxable acres. The net result of the above formula is that some taxpayers would have to pay more in local taxes while others would pay less. The New Jersey recommendation also avoids the problem of balancing the benefits derived from exempt facilities against the municipal services rendered to them, but it should be considered by various jurisdictions throughout the nation as a possible approach to the problem of tax-exempt properties at a time when there is general restiveness over the issue.

A study similar to that of the Apy Commission was made in 1967 by the Ontario, Canada, Committee on Taxation.

Its report, published in three volumes, made the following points, among others.

> We find little to justify burdening all property owners with the cost of the relief given to places of worship in recognition of the indirect benefits they confer upon society generally. If we accept as a fact that there is little prospect of public acceptance for direct subsidy [to churches], the problem we face is that the continued full exemption of places of worship unfairly saddles local property owners with the full burden of the tax relief given to churches.

The Ontario study offered six arguments against exemption: (1) Exemptions narrow the tax base, thereby increasing the tax load on owners of taxable property; (2) a tax exemption is an indirect subsidy, the cost of which is not generally apparent, and it is subject to less control than a grant, which ordinarily is renewable annually; (3) tax exemption may not distribute a government subsidy in the most equitable or desirable manner; (4) the proportion of all properties in the community that are exempt varies from one municipality to another, thereby creating disproportionate burdens among local communities; (5) exemptions are for the most part legislated by the province (state), but their burden falls on municipalities and local school boards; (6) exemptions, once established, are not readily terminated, and thus they tend to perpetuate community wishes of an earlier day. In addition, the range and extent of exemptions can grow well beyond justifiable limits.

However, the Ontario study does make the following observation:

> We nevertheless hold the view that the indirect benefits to society that flow from places of worship justify some

measure of relief from local taxation. We do not believe that there should be full exemption, because, in our view, church members who directly benefit from local government services should contribute to their costs. What this contribution should be is essentially a matter of judgment and we think it should be perhaps one-half the normal tax. We realize, however, that a sudden change from complete exemption of places of worship to 50 per cent taxation would impose tremendous hardship on churches with limited financial resources. We therefore propose that the change be made in stages over several years . . .

The Ontario Committee on Taxation, whose report was subsequently backed by the Metro Executive Committee of Toronto, recommended that churches and religious seminaries (not classed as institutions of higher learning or as private schools) be reassessed at actual value and taxed at 5 percent the first year and 10 percent the second year, with increases of 5 percent each succeeding year until the level of 35 percent had been reached. The figure of 35 percent, added the authors of the study, would be subject to review and raised or lowered wherever it was deemed appropriate.

A curious aspect of the argument for church tax exemption is that such exemptions are forbidden by the constitutions of forty-four states in the U. S., as witness the following excerpts therefrom.

ALABAMA: . . . *no one shall be compelled by law . . . to pay any . . . taxes . . . for maintaining any minister or ministry . . .*

ALASKA: *No law shall be made respecting an establishment of religion, or prohibiting the free exercise thereof.*

ARIZONA: [Bars the use of taxes or public funds "in aid of any church."]

ARKANSAS: . . . *no man can, of right, be compelled to . . . support any place of worship . . .*

CALIFORNIA: [Prohibits public funds "or anything" to be given to or in aid of any religious sect, church.]

COLORADO: *No persons shall be required to . . . support any ministry or place of worship, religious sect or denomination . . .*

CONNECTICUT: . . . *no person shall by law be compelled to . . . support . . . any congregation, church, or religious association.*

DELAWARE: . . . *no man shall or ought to be compelled to . . . contribute to the erection or support of any place of worship, or to the maintenance of any ministry . . .*

FLORIDA: [Bars use of public funds to aid any church or sect.]

GEORGIA: [Forbids use of public money to aid churches or "any sectarian institution."]

HAWAII: *No law shall be enacted respecting an establishment of religion or prohibiting the free exercise thereof . . .*

IDAHO: *No person shall be required to . . . support any ministry or place of worship, religious sect or denomination . . .*

ILLINOIS: *No person shall be required to . . . support any ministry or place of worship . . .*

INDIANA: [Prohibits use of public money for the support of religious institutions.]

IOWA: . . . *nor shall any person be compelled to . . . pay taxes for building or repairing places of worship, or the maintenance of any minister, or ministry.*

KANSAS: . . . *nor shall any person be compelled to . . . support . . . any form of worship.*

KENTUCKY: . . . . *nor shall any person be compelled to . . . contribute to the erection or maintenance of any such place* [of worship] *or to the salary or support of any minister of religion.*

LOUISIANA: *No money shall ever be taken from the public treasury, directly or indirectly, in aid of any church, sect, or denomination or religion, or in aid of any priest, minister or teacher thereof, as such.*

MARYLAND: . . . *nor ought any person be compelled to contribute . . . to maintain any place of worship . . .*

MASSACHUSETTS: *and no such grant, appropriation or use of public money or property or loan of public credit shall be made or authorized for the purpose of founding, maintaining or aiding any church, religious denomination or society.*

MICHIGAN: *No person shall be compelled . . . to contribute to the erection or support of any place of religious worship, or to pay . . . taxes . . . for the support of any minister of the gospel . . .*

MINNESOTA: . . . *nor shall any man be compelled to . . . support any place of worship, or to maintain any religious or ecclesiastical ministry . . .*

MISSISSIPPI: [Forbids any grant or donation or gratuity "for a sectarian purpose or use."]

MISSOURI: [Bars use of state funds to aid any church or sect.]

MONTANA: *No person shall be required to . . . support any ministry.*

NEBRASKA: *No person shall be compelled . . . to support any place of worship.*

NEVADA: [Bars use of public funds for "sectarian purpose."]

NEW MEXICO: *No person shall be required to . . . support any religious sect or denomination.*

OHIO: *No person shall be compelled to . . . support any place of worship . . .*

OKLAHOMA: *No public money or property shall ever be appropriated . . . for the use, benefit, or support of any sect, church, denomination or system of religion . . .*

OREGON: [Bars appropriations of public funds "for the benefit of any religious, or theological institution."]

PENNSYLVANIA: *. . . no man can of right be compelled to . . . support any place of worship, or to maintain any ministry . . .*

RHODE ISLAND: *No man shall be compelled to . . . support any place of worship, or to maintain any ministry . . .*

SOUTH CAROLINA: *The General Assembly shall make no law respecting an establishment of religion or prohibiting the free exercise thereof.*

SOUTH DAKOTA: *No person shall be compelled to support any ministry or place of worship . . . No money or property of the state shall be given or appropriated for the benefit of any sectarian or religious society or institution.*

TENNESSEE: *. . . no man can of right be compelled to attend, erect, or support any place of worship, or to maintain any minister against his consent.*

TEXAS: *No money shall be appropriated or drawn from the treasury for the benefit of any sect or religious society, theological or religious seminary; nor shall prop-*

erty belonging to the state be appropriated for such purposes.

UTAH: *There shall be no union of Church and State, nor shall any church dominate the State or interfere.*

VERMONT: *No man ought to, or of right can be compelled to . . . support any place of worship . . .*

VIRGINIA: *No man shall be compelled to . . . support any religious worship . . . And the General Assembly shall not . . . pass any law . . . or the people of any district within this State . . . levy on themselves or others any tax for the erection of repair of any house of public worship, or for the support of any church . . .*

WASHINGTON: *No public money or property shall be appropriated for, or applied to any religious worship, exercise or instruction, or the support of any religious establishment.*

WEST VIRGINIA: *No man shall be compelled to . . . support any religious worship, place or ministry whatsoever . . .*

WISCONSIN: *. . . nor shall any man be compelled to . . . erect or support any place of worship, or to maintain any ministry . . . , nor shall any money be drawn from the treasury for the benefit of religion, societies of religion or theological seminaries.*

WYOMING: [Bars use of state money to aid any sectarian or religious society or institution.]

Notwithstanding these prohibitions, every one of the above-mentioned states does, in practice, provide tax exemptions to the church. This is also true of cities all over the country. Let us look at a selected sample of cities and see what the property holdings of the Catholic Church are, in terms of what can be elicited from official municipal records and other reliable sources of data.*

Though the Catholic population of Washington, D.C., does not exceed 10 percent of the city's total population, Catholic institutions own nearly 60 percent of all religious properties in the capital that are used by Christian denominations. Washington's Catholic churches and their attached schools have an assessed valuation of upwards of $77 million; this includes the National Shrine of the Immaculate Conception, valued at $12.4 million. In addition to a dozen private and diocesan elementary and secondary schools, the Catholic Church runs an extensive operation that includes universities, colleges, academies, seminaries, monasteries, convents, retreats and other properties. These include Georgetown University, with an assessed valuation of $22.8 million; Catholic University of America, $24.5 million; Trinity College, $7 million; Dunbarton College, $2.8 million; Sisters of Visitation, $2.2 million; St. John's College, $2 million; Sisters of Providence, $1.9 million; Catholic Sisters College, $1.2 million; and Gonzaga College, $1 million. Two Catholic hospitals, Georgetown and Providence, are respectively assessed at $11.9 million and $5.3 million. Washington's Catholic Charities, assessed at $5.8 million, consists primarily of monasteries, nunneries and correctional institutions. Included in this category is the headquarters of the National Catholic Welfare Conference (the political center of American Catholic activity), assessed at $1.1 million.

The Hartford, Connecticut, Archdiocese, with 812,011 communicants, or about half of the 1.6-million population, owns 47.5 percent of the total assessed religious property, at a worth of $36.8 million. According to Borden V. Mahoney, a city official who supplied information on Hartford's tax base,

* The author is especially grateful to Dr. Martin A. Larson of Phoenix, Arizona, who corroborated the figures for the remainder of this chapter.

the Catholic church buildings are assessed at $14.2 million, the hospitals at $12 million. Parochial schools are assessed at $4.8 million, and the parish houses and rectories at $3 million. Fifteen convents and monasteries are evaluated at $1.8 million for tax purposes. The House of the Good Shepherd has a $919,-130 assessment, while the Mount St. Benedict Cemetery is valued at $88,060. There are no Catholic colleges or seminaries in Hartford.

In Pittsburgh, Pennsylvania, the Roman Catholic Church has seventy-eight parishes and eighty elementary and secondary schools. The churches are assessed at $27.6 million, while the parochial schools, charities and convents are valued at $6.9 million. The other schools and universities have been assessed at $16.1 million; this figure includes Duquesne University ($12.8 million), Mount Mercy College ($1.8 million), Catholic Institute ($1.2 million) and St. Paul Seminary ($325,196). Catholic hospitals in Pittsburgh have a worth of $20 million, while the cemeteries show $826,190 as their valuation. The total of these properties comes to $71.5 million and represents 57 percent of the property of all Pittsburgh's churches combined.

Inasmuch as the Catholics are in political control of St. Paul, Minnesota, bond issues dealing with projected constructions of new public schools have been defeated over and over again. This may explain why assessments on Catholic churches and attached schools have risen 47.3 percent in the last few years to a total of $9.8 million, whereas the assessments on public schools have dropped from $6.8 million to $4.3 million. The figures given here are for Ramsey County, which includes the city of St. Paul and its immediate environs. They show that total Catholic real estate is valued at $22.1 million, or 50.3 percent of the total religious property. In St. Paul Catholic priests run forty-six churches, forty-five schools and four colleges and seminaries. The Cathedral of St. Paul is assessed at $853,-

820. This church and all its sister churches, with their attached schools, have a combined assessment of $11.9 million. Their true value, however, is appraised at $92 million by both Leonard L. Peterson, principal clerk in the Office of the Assessor, and Horace Contini, chief clerk in the Office of Records. Following are some of the properties belonging to the Catholic Church, with respective assessments: St. Paul's Priory and School, $2 million; St. Joseph's Hospital, $1.5 million; College of St. Thomas, $1.4 million; College of St. Catherine, $992,-910; Nazareth Hall Seminary, $884,200; St. Paul's Seminary, $603,320; and an orphanage, $596,830. Based on official computations, it is known that although the estimated values of Catholic property in Ramsey County are put at more than $22 million, the actual value of this real estate comes to $176.8 million.

Unlike its sister city across the river, Minneapolis is predominantly Scandinavian Protestant. The Catholics own 29.2 percent of the assessed religious properties—which comes to a figure of $24.2 million. Among the thirty-seven Catholic churches and their adjoining schools, which reach $11.8 million in assessed valuations, are the Basilica of St. Mary, assessed at $959,000, and the Church of the Annunciation, at $871,300. The only Catholic hospital in Minneapolis is St. Mary's, which carries an assessment of $5.9 million.

Catholic holdings in Portland, Oregon, are assessed at $54 million, a figure that represents 38.3 percent of the total religious property of the city. In terms of its two-million population, metropolitan Portland has a low ratio of Catholic communicants—200,000.

The city of St. Louis, Missouri, was founded in 1762 by French trading merchants from New Orleans. Its metropolitan area has a Catholic population of 511,669, or nearly 27 percent of the 1.9 million residents. The Catholic-owned property is 52.3 percent of the total religious property, and it amounts to $56.1 million. Of this, St. Louis University, a Jesuit-owned school, is assessed at $14.1 million, but figures supplied by Oliver Dippold, supervisor of property appraisers, reveal the official book value to be $72 million. Although St. Louis University, according to its charter, is not supposed to operate tax-free commercial properties, the school has purchased apartment buildings, hotels and other real estate and is using them as dorms, thereby dropping the buildings from the tax rolls.

The Catholic Church in St. Louis has seventy-nine parishes and sixty-seven elementary and secondary schools. The assessed value of the archdiocese's churches and attached schools is $6.8 million. Nine Catholic hospitals carry a combined assessment of $8.7 million. The Catholics also have various missions like Father Dempsey's Hotels, a Girls Industrial Home, the Hospice of Alverne, the Augustinian Friars Monastery and the convent of the Franciscan Sisters—all of which have a total assessment of $2.7 million. Under the name of the late Joseph Cardinal Ritter there are 154 pieces of property which have received an assessed value of over $11.4 million. Catholic cemeteries in St. Louis show $3.5 million in assessments.

As the dominant denomination, the Catholics in Cleveland, Ohio, run 119 parishes, 112 parochial schools, seventeen high schools, four seminaries, seven hospitals and three colleges, in addition to a complex of monasteries, convents, homes, protective institutions and other facilities. The Cathedral of St. John the Evangelist, a rectory, the diocesan center and St. John's College, which are located on what is known as Cathedral Square, have a combined assessment of $4.1 million. Churches in other parts of the city are St. Ignatius (assessed at $1.2 million), St. Stanislaus ($1 million) and the Holy Name ($1 million). All the churches and parochial schools in Cleveland have an assessed valuation of $43.2 million—but according to officials in Cleveland's Board of Revision and Tax Assessments, the true combined value of the aforementioned properties runs to something like $135 million. Four Catholic hospitals and a number of convents, monasteries, retirement homes and correctional institutions have a combined assessment of $15 million. The Catholic cemeteries there are valued at $617,460. The total of Cleveland's Catholic-held properties comes to $74.4 million, representing 57.8 percent of the city's religious property. This total does not include two Catholic colleges, John Carroll University and Ursuline College, which are just outside Cleveland and which together are worth in the vicinity of $15 million. Cleveland's Catholics number 340,000 in a total population of about 815,000.

Buffalo, New York, received several waves of Catholic immigrants between 1840 and 1920, most of them from Poland, Ireland, Italy, Germany, Czechoslovakia and Hungary. The statistics show that Roman Catholics make up a little over half of the population. In Buffalo there are seventy-two parishes, which administer ninety elementary schools, six colleges and one seminary. Like most cities, Buffalo is deeply concerned over the fact that so many organizations enjoy a tax-exempt status. The city assessor's books reveal that there is over $91.8 million worth of tax-exempt properties belonging to religious institutions. The value of Catholic property comes to approximately $67 million, or 73 percent of all religious property.

In Buffalo most of the exempt properties belonging to religious groups are undervalued. For instance, the Mount St. Joseph Academy, with buildings and land worth about $8 million, is assessed at $1.5 million, whereas Canisius College, with a physical plant worth approximately $15 million, carries an assessment of $4.5 million.

Some of Buffalo's Catholic properties cannot be identified separately, because they are lumped together under the diocese. For instance, Buffalo's largest diocesan high schools, McMahon, Ryan, Carroll, Timon, Colton, Fallon and Daugherty, are not distinguished as schools on the city's tax rolls. The following, however, appear on the rolls: Canisius College ($4.5 million), D'Youville College ($3.7 million), Institute of St. Joseph ($1.8 million), St. Mary's School for the Deaf ($1.4 million), and Canisius High School ($1.3 million). One tax expert calculated that the actual worth of Catholic property in Buffalo was $250 million.

Baltimore, Maryland, was for many years the center of American Catholicism, and although it is now predominantly Protestant, many of the citizens feel that the city is "run by the Catholics." The Catholics make up about 34 percent of the religious affiliates in the city, but their total tax-exempt wealth is put at 51.4 percent. Compare this with the Protestant figures of 55.3 percent of the affiliates and 33.4 percent of the tax-exempt wealth. George M. Downs of the Statistical Division of Baltimore's Department of Assessments made available the figures on Catholic property. The Cathedral of Mary Our Queen, which was built at a cost of nearly $12 million, is assessed at $6.9 million. The seventy parish churches and their fifty-nine schools, together with some other elementary and secondary schools, have a combined assessment of $49.4 million—an average of $705,000 for each parish. Since the true value of Catholic real estate in Baltimore is not less than $160 million, the holdings for each parish average about $2.3 million.

Providence, Rhode Island, long a Baptist-Quaker city, underwent a change of complexion after 1840, when great numbers of Catholic immigrants began to settle there. Today the Roman Catholics in the Providence Diocese maintain twenty-eight parish churches and twenty-six elementary and secondary schools. Catholic property in this city, according to Louis Cote, assessor, represents 68.7 percent of the total religious property held and has an assessed value of $38.8 million.

Bishop Russell J. McVinney, who has been chief pastor of

the Providence Diocese for over twenty years, is an example of a clergyman who understands the intricacies and subtleties of public relations, and to his credit, he is a fine practitioner of the art. For example, when the diocese opened a new $2.2-million three-story office building of aluminum and glass at Cathedral Square, Bishop McVinney was quick to announce that the Church would renounce part of the tax exemption to which it was entitled and would give the city a yearly sum of $10,000. The normal tax levy for the new structure would have been $56,760. Bishop McVinney let it be known that his voluntary payment was "fitting and proper" in view of the city's desperate need for new sources of revenue. He also took the occasion to let people know that the Catholic parishes of Providence do indeed pay taxes and that they had paid the city a total of $59,758 in taxes on rectories and convents, even though he felt that the convents should be tax-exempt because they produce no income whatever and were "a drain."

Although usually very little publicity is given to the fact that most Catholic Church businesses do not pay taxes on their profits, occasionally a complaint that this constitutes unfair competition does get into the newspapers, especially when a large sum of money is involved. Such was the case of Technology, Inc., of Dayton, Ohio.

In July 1965 Maurice Krug, president of Technology, Inc., lodged a formal complaint with the U. S. Air Force on the grounds that his company had lost a half-million-dollar Air Force contract to a Catholic organization which came under the umbrella of tax exemption. Technology, Inc.'s bid was about $10,000 higher than that of the University of Dayton on a contract to gather data on the effects of stress on C-141 jet transport planes. The University of Dayton, which is owned and operated by the Society of Mary, had military contracts totaling more than $3.6 million, placing it 125th in the list of prime contractors for the U.S. Defense Department.

"The federal taxes our firm would have paid on the $500,000 contract," Mr. Krug said, "would have been much more than the $10,000 less bid made by the University of Dayton. It is unfair to ask a private company which pays taxes to bid against a nonprofit organization which pays none." He also made it known that Dayton U. got vast amounts of equipment from the government at no cost, whereas his company had to buy everything and still pay taxes on any profit made.

The manner in which some Catholic organizations use their tax-exempt status has a tendency to irk their competitors and the non-Catholic taxpaying community. What happened in New Britain, Connecticut, is a case in point. In 1939 the Archdiocese of Hartford purchased for $23,500 a 121.5-acre tract of unused land in nearby New Britain that formerly belonged to attorney Patrick F. McDonough. In order to avoid paying real-estate taxes on the land, the archbishop had a body buried on the premises so that it would be technically listed as a cemetery. Twenty-seven years later, when the price of real estate in the area had zoomed, the archdiocese removed the single body, enabling the Catholic Cemetery Association of New Britain, Inc., to sell the land to Mayor Paul J. Manafort for city use. The selling price was $607,500—a profit of $584,000, not including the saving of $200,000 in taxes over the years.

6

ALMIGHTY DOLLAR, AMEN!

To make and extort money in every shape that can be devised, and at the same time to decry its value seems to have become an epidemical disease.—GEORGE WASHINGTON

THE "CRY PAX" COLUMN which appears on the front page of the *National Catholic Reporter* is subtitled "A Column Without Rules" because it pokes gentle and often satirical fun at oddities of the ecclesiastic establishment (many of the contributions come from anonymous priests). Several years ago the following item appeared there.

> A circular from B. C. Ziegler & Company announced an offering of $4,500,000 in direct obligation serial notes, guaranteed by a corporation having assets in excess of $115,000,000, a net worth reported at $86,000,000, and a five-year annual cash operation gain of $5,190,302, or three times the maximum annual interest on all its funded debt. The guarantor: The Poor Sisters of St. Francis Seraph of the Perpetual Adoration, Province of the Immaculate Heart of Mary, Mishawaka, Indiana.

The *Reporter* added its own comment in italics: *"Mishawaka is a long way from Assisi."*

The circular from the B. C. Ziegler company is typical of those put out by some fifty underwriting firms that specialize in arranging financing for church expansions. These firms, some of which handle only Catholic organizations, annually market $100 million worth of institutional bonds. The underwriters generally buy an entire bond issue from a church by bidding slightly less than the face value of the securities, then reoffer the bonds to individual investors at higher prices. To prospective buyers the underwriting firms issue detailed prospectuses. Other firms known as "financial program supervisors" may take on a sale for a church at a fee sometimes as low as $800. These commercial houses might print $100,000 in bonds, handle some legal work and provide sales brochures, but the church itself must take on the responsibility of peddling the bonds. Still others, known as "best-effort firms," provide more promotional assistance and sometimes locate prospective investors, but don't guarantee to sell any bonds. There are also a few companies that provide a combination of such services and sometimes even underwrite a portion of a church bond issue, at fees ranging up to about $4,000 for a $100,000 underwriting.

Though a number of states have tightened their control over bonds issued by charitable organizations, the practice still goes on. Bond issues by Catholic organizations which ordinarily keep their business operations secret often provide a good clue to the institutions' assets and worth. For example, take the first-mortgage serial-bonds issue which the Mercy Hospital of Canton, Ohio, run by a nonprofit corporation of Roman Catholic sisters, offered on February 1, 1970, through the assistance of B. C. Ziegler & Company. The prospectus states that Mercy Hospital, incorporated March 9, 1926, owns and operates the 200-bed hospital in downtown Canton and the new 238-bed Timken Mercy Hospital, located on a thirty-two-acre estate which was donated to the Sisters of Charity of

St. Augustine in 1950. The corporation, which also operates a nurses' school at the downtown hospital, is engaged in a large expansion and improvement program at its Timken Mercy Hospital. Upon completion of the latter the old Mercy Hospital will be closed, the property sold and the nursing school moved to the new site. The program, estimated to cost approximately $13.2 million, will provide 350 beds in a new ten-story wing, expanded ancillary services and a new nursing school for 185 student nurses. The bonds authorized were for $6 million and were to mature on November 1, 1977.

For security against default on the bonds, the Sisters of Charity have tied up approximately $19 million in their Canton operation. The book value of the land and the land improvements is listed as $112,200, existing buildings and equipment as $5.7 million, new construction as $11.8 million and new equipment as $1.3 million. The audited balance sheet of the corporation as of December 31, 1968, its statement of income and expense for the four years then ended and a balance sheet and operating statement for the year ended December 31, 1969, are set forth in the prospectus. The balance sheets reflect total assets of $18.4 million and fund balances (net worth) of $14 million. The net incomes were $307,987 for 1965; $484,492 for 1966; $431,154 for 1967; $528,879 for 1968; and $681,835 for 1969.

The same underwriting firm, B. C. Ziegler & Company, issued a prospectus for the St. Jude Hospital of Fullerton, California, a 230-bed hospital run by the Sisters of St. Joseph of Orange, who, through three civil corporations, also own seven other hospitals in California and one in Texas. The purpose of issuing direct obligation serial notes was to expand and improve St. Jude Hospital at a cost of approximately $6 million. To raise $4 million, the corporation provided the usual security by agreeing not to mortgage any of its property. The book value of the land, buildings and equipment was listed as follows: land, $45,300; existing buildings and equipment, $4.6 million; new construction and equipment, $6 million. The corporation's balance sheet showed total assets of $10 million, a net worth of $6 million and a total funded indebtedness of $1.2 million. As set forth in the prospectuses, the net incomes were $612,122 for 1966, $536,869 for 1967, $735,012 for 1968, and $971,884 for 1969. During the four years, therefore, the corporation's total income was more than $2.8 million.

Ordinarily, bond issues by the Catholic Church do not make the newspapers, but several years ago the Sisters of St. Joseph hit the financial pages of Toronto's dailies when the organization floated a bond issue of $12 million. It was one of the largest money-raising ventures of its type ever reported in Canada. The Sisters backed up their bonds with 34 percent of their assets in the Toronto Archdiocese—St. Joseph's and St. Michael's Hospitals, a mother house and a home for the aged. For some reason newspapers in the United States seem more reluctant to publish information presented in bond prospectuses. There was, for example, no mention in a newspaper when in 1967 the Boston Archdiocese revealed assets of $635,-891,004 on a bond prospectus.

Below are the asset figures of twenty-three Catholic women's orders as reported by recent bond prospectuses. Needless to say, if one wanted to make some calculations, one could come up with a pretty good estimate of the probable total wealth of America's Catholic women's orders, give or take a few million dollars.

	Millions
Sisters of the Holy Cross	$110.9
Sisters of the Sorrowful Mother	93.6
Sisters of Charity of Providence	90.1
Sisters of Mercy, Omaha Province	75.6

Sisters of Charity	66.5
Sisters of Mercy	39.7
Sisters of Charity, Grey Nuns	34.9
Little Sisters of the Poor	25.0
Dominican Sisters	24.3
Sisters of St. Francis of Assisi	18.2
Sisters of St. Joseph of Newark	17.9
Sisters of Charity of St. Elizabeth	16.0
Sisters of St. Joseph of Concordia	13.3
Sisters of St. Francis of Buffalo	13.2
Sisters of St. Joseph	11.8
Sisters of Loretto	11.4
Missionary Sisters, Servants of the Holy Spirit	11.4
Dominican Sisters of St. Catherine of Siena of Kenosha	7.8
California Institute of the Sisters of the Immaculate Heart	7.3
Sisters of Christian Charity, Wilmette	6.4
Benedictine Sisters	3.7
Congregation of the Third Order of St. Dominic of St. Mary	3.6
Grey Nuns of Charity	3.0

Like all other legitimate business organizations, including Protestant and Jewish groups, the Catholic Church scrupulously sticks to the limitations of the local laws in issuing bonds. There are no instances in which its bond issues have failed to adhere to existing statutes, nor are any of the other business gimmicks used by the Church illegal in the strict, technical sense. However, there are certain loopholes which can legitimately be exploited.

The "lease-back" operation, also referred to as "bootstrapping" or "purchase and lease-back," has been a very popular and useful device for the Church. This is how it works: A church finds or is offered a successful business and purchases it. Usually the purchase price is the most generous possible appraisal of what the business is worth. The church then leases the assets to a completely new corporation, which often turns out to be the original owners. Under the leasing agreement, the new corporation gives the church 80 percent of its profits and winds up having to pay taxes on only 20 percent. But the church, which still has to pay off annually its debt to the sellers, uses the 80 percent profits it receives from the business. It may keep 8 percent of the profit income for itself and pay 72 percent to the original owners, who are now operating the company on a leasing agreement. This means that the original owners (now tenants) can report the 72 percent as capital gains and pay only about one half or less in taxes of what they would be required to pay if it were all business income. In other words, the church has put up exactly $0.00 in cash and pays off the business with money not subject to taxation. It is a somewhat complicated procedure—but all perfectly legal.

The magazine *Christianity Today* explains another tax device: "Suppose a church buys a $1-million business that, in view of tax exemptions, shows an annual profit of $120,000. It can borrow $800,000 to purchase the business at the preferred loan rate of 4 percent, or $32,000. Hence, on an investment of $200,000 the church will net $88,000, or 44 percent."

Let us look at another example. At the end of twenty years the depreciation allowance on a hotel worth $1 million is almost exhausted. At this point, the corporation that owns the hotel must pay full federal taxes on all net operating revenue, which means that the annual profit is cut down by $50,000. In another twenty years this would total to $1 million and would mean a difference of $500,000 in net income. So the corporation sells the hotel for $1 million to a church, a tax-exempt organization. The corporation accepts a down payment of $100,000 from the church, which through mortgage financing gets a loan of $900,000. The firm then leases back the hotel from the church at an annual rental of $75,000, which in addition to insurance, repairs and taxes is deductible. The church pays off the mortgage at $67,360 a year for twenty years, at the end of which it will own the property. Meanwhile, it has recovered not only the original investment but also another $52,800. When the mortgage is liquidated, the church has a tax-exempt income of $75,000 a year without having invested any money. The former owner (the corporation) may now repurchase the property for $1 million, giving the church a tax-free capital gain, and repeat the process of depreciation. In another twenty years the church would show a net profit of $1.3 million, and the corporation would have a cash advantage of about $500,000.

In a recent lease-back transaction the Diocese of Austin, Texas, purchased twenty-two nursing homes in Massachusetts for approximately $4.7 million—one of the largest real-estate deals in the state's history. As soon as the transaction was completed, Bishop L. J. Reicher leased the properties back to the original owners, Geriatrics Management, Inc., of Milton.

An explanation of the lease-back operation is provided by Ferdinand Lundberg in his book *The Rich and the Super-Rich*.*

> Let us suppose that an original investment of $10 million was now valued at $100 million. If it were sold, it would incur a capital gains tax of approximately $22.5 million. But if it were all given to a foundation, the foundation could sell it and pay no gains tax. Now if the foundation lends the whole sum back to the donor at 1 per cent, he pays it $1 million a year. And if he makes $3 million on a tax-free investment in government bonds, he keeps $2 million annually, tax free. But if he had sold the original amount, he would have had only $77.5 million after-tax capital which, invested at 5 per cent, would have brought him $3,875,000. After payment of about

* Published by Lyle Stuart, Inc., New York, 1968.

$2,172,500 (or 70 per cent) income tax, he would have remaining $1,162,500 annually or almost half less than by the first procedure.

Mr. Lundberg's reference to the "foundation" brings up still another method by which churches can realize savings and profits. The Catholic Church has found that a small foundation is useful in all sorts of secret business affairs, as Mr. Lundberg has pointed out. There are more than 15,000 foundations in the United States, and the number is increasing each year. The Catholic Church, like thousands of other organizations, has joined the parade of foundational activity that has proliferated since the enactment of the income-tax and estate-tax laws. The foundations are exempt not only from income taxes but also from capital-gains taxes, and these attractive features have not escaped the attention of archbishops seeking to escape taxes.

Foundations provide the Catholic Church with a way of keeping control of wealth even while the wealth itself is being given away. Under Section 501 (c) (3) of the Internal Revenue Code, a foundation may not engage in active business, although it may own controlling interest in corporations that do so. Within the prescription of the law, foundations can, therefore, receive passive income in the form of rentals, lease payments, royalties, interest, dividends, and capital gains without tax liability. True, a foundation's income must eventually go to charity, but there can be a long time lag between income and disbursement. Apart from the competitive advantages, the foundations enjoy a lack of government supervision, while serving a variety of business purposes for their principal grantor.

A corporation wishing to liquidate an investment can use a foundation as a tax-free receptacle for whatever capital gain is involved, by turning the investment over to a foundation and having the foundation dispose of it; in this operation there is no gift tax and no capital-gains tax to be paid. Now the foundation may lend the full liquid sum to the donor corporation at a nominal interest rate. Or the foundation may use the proceeds to buy a major block of stock in a company that the donor corporation wants to control; this maneuver is often effected by using the money that ordinarily would have been slated for taxes.

Foundations, of course, are neither a creation nor a monopoly of the Catholic Church. But they are a welcome and useful apparatus in the financial structure of a number of archdioceses and dioceses. Exactly how many Catholic-owned foundations there are in America no one knows. The annual *Catholic Almanac*, which lists by name virtually every organization affiliated with the religion, does not list Catholic foundations *per se* under any category or in the index. It is therefore impossible to give any kind of cumulative report on these Church-controlled foundations. Nevertheless, let us look at one such foundation for which detailed information has been acquired. The Catholic Foundation of Dallas, Texas, may not be typical of other Catholic foundations throughout the contry, but it does give an insight into how such a structure performs in the world of business.

At the annual meeting of its board of trustees on April 22, 1969, Frank H. Heller, president of the Catholic Foundation, reviewing the organization's operations for the calendar year 1968, reported that it had "made significant progress." He listed the total assets as $986,854 and compared them with the previous year's figure of $844,027. With $111,587 on hand or in banks, the foundation reported it had marketable securities valued at $566,355. The previous year the securities had totaled $227,978. During 1968 the total contributions and income received were $296,170, contrasted with the 1967 figure of $339,002. Total expenses for 1968 came to $72,036, the biggest item being $26,130 in interest payments. The report also traced the foundation's net-worth growth since 1962, when the year-end figure was $28,389. Although the total slid down for three years, it began to move upward in 1966 and by the end of that year it was $434,336. A year later it was placed at $738,869, and by 1968 the sum had reached over $960,000.

The foundation's report devoted seven pages to giving the financial picture of the Christ the King Church Corporation of Dallas and its project, Billy Martin's Carriage House in Washington, D.C. It gave the corporation's fixed assets as $467,982 and its total assets as $820,466. The restaurant project in Washington had at the end of February 1969 a gross profit of $1,099,438, as compared to a gross profit of $1,095,004 for the preceding period. Acquired by the Dallas organization in 1965, the Carriage House, one of the finest restaurants in the nation's capital, showed a cash balance of $199,753 at the end of February 1969, after the corporation in Texas had withdrawn $233,462 from the total cash available. Except for a District of Columbia franchise tax amounting to $16,244, general taxes amounting to $4,133 and payroll taxes amounting to $18,493, the report does not itemize the payment of any other direct taxes.

Included in the report also was a balance sheet on the Cathedral Foundation, Trust B (Thomas K. Gorman, trustee). Total assets from this operation came to $966,476, of which $960,743 were oil production payments. The oil production payments in the year previous to the report came to more than $1.3 million. The net income from this oil production was put at $61,317 for 1968 and $81,823 for 1967, but after distributions the final totals were reduced to $215 and $1,071 for the two respective years.

Operating quite differently from the Catholic Foundation of Dallas are three other Catholic-controlled foundations, the

118

University Hill Foundation, De Rance Incorporated, and the Catholic Seminary Foundation. As a "feeder" for Loyola of Los Angeles, the University Hill Foundation has an interest in about twenty-five separate businesses. These include three sand, gravel and concrete companies, a foundry, a plastics enterprise, three dairies, a hotel, a window-making factory, a printing plant and businesses engaged in the sale of locks, oil burners and rubber products. De Rance Incorporated of Milwaukee serves as a feeder foundation for several Roman Catholic religious orders. The company owns nearly 30 percent of Miller Beer, the eighth-largest beer producer in the United States, which reports total sales of nearly $150 million each year. The Catholic Seminary Foundation of Indianapolis is carrying out plans, under a ten-year project, to rebuild a four-square-mile area with low- to moderate-income homes; in all, a total of $250 million will be invested. The Reverend Mario Shaw, the foundation's executive administrator, explains to prospective house buyers that under flexible interest rates and rules laid down by the 1968 Housing Act, a family can buy one of the foundation's houses for as little as fifty dollars a month.

Another means of avoiding taxes is the "corporation sole," which allows a bishop to hold, in his own name as bishop and without paying taxes, as much real estate, stocks, bonds, mortgages, cash and other property as he can amass—there is no legal limitation. The bishop may manage these assets in whatever manner he wishes, as if they were his personal wealth. Since the theory is that he is acting as an agent of the Church, there is no tax liability and he is not required to divulge any figures or other information. According to law, all the property held under corporation sole passes automatically to a bishop's successor without any need for formal transfer. Thus, as a corporation sole, the bishop is not answerable to any authority—federal, state or city—as to the management, use or disposition of whatever wealth he gains title to. Nor is he required to make any report to the priests or laymen in his jurisdiction, even though the latter may have contributed the wherewithal for a corporation sole to accumulate these material things. A variation of this, also very legal, is the "corporation aggregate," in which the title is nominally vested in a board, but since the bishop appoints the members of the board, over which he also presides, the end result is virtually the same.

Another method used in Catholic business operations is the "business front." This is created by a church which lends some money to a partnership. The latter forthwith pays heavy interest (deductible on the partnership tax return) and makes a substantial deductible contribution to the parent church organization. Often the business can be made to prosper if the priests are asked by their superiors to urge the parishioners to patronize the particular business in question. It should be pointed out that in most cases of a loan to a given partnership, the rate of interest is an exceedingly high one.

Still another tax device is the "Clay Brown operation," which works like this: A Catholic order or diocese buys a thriving business at an inflated figure. Usually no money is invested, but in some cases a small sum might be involved. The notes are paid off out of current income. The former owner of the business is now the manager, and the money he is paid comes under the classification of lightly taxed capital gains—whereas before it was in the category of heavily taxed earned income. Moreover, the manager has no Social Security to pay, and from his untaxed capital gains he can build an estate rapidly.

It is interesting to note that this so-called Clay Brown operation, which is now quite a popular gimmick with charities, came about as a result of a case adjudicated by the U. S. Supreme Court in April 1965. The Clay B. Brown lumber con-

cern of Fortuna, California, had "sold" itself to a cancer research outfit for $1.3 million. The down payment was five
thousand dollars, with the remainder to be paid over a ten-
year period. The Clay B. Brown company then became
known as Fortuna Mills and leased back the facility, agreeing
to pay 80 percent of its operating profits to the cancer organization, which in turn agreed to pay 90 percent of what it realized from Fortuna to Clay B. Brown stockholders in payment for the mill. The Supreme Court decided that Fortuna
Mills did not have to pay corporation taxes and that it could
treat all profits from the sale as capital gains, taxable at a low
rate. This decision turned out to be a godsend for all religious
groups, for it provided them with a tax shelter.

Although the "Clay Brown Operation" and other favorite
ploys are strictly within the law, they edge users into the
twilight area of the moral, raising the question of what is,
ethically, right and what is wrong. But the quest for the dollar,
The Almighty Dollar, is manifestly another value in that it is
the object of universal devotion. Given that money is the route
to all evil, some clerics are right there in the swim.

Some clerics have very few scruples about what they do to
make money. Fortunately they are a small minority, but the
Church, any church, would be better off without them. In the
last twenty years a number of ambiguous "priestlike" individuals have used the U. S. Postal System to reap a quick but
questionable dollar. Any Catholic who becomes known as an
"easy-mark contributor" to charitable causes will soon discover that his name has been included on many of the
Church's mailing lists, a few of which have passed into the
hands of the wrong people. For some Catholics it is not un-
common to receive four or five appeals a month, or even more
during December. Though most Catholic appeals are legitimate and deserving, some of them are not. Posing behind fake
Church titles, some unscrupulous operators use most of the

contributions for their operating expenses and for paying themselves overly generous commissions. These operations of dubious integrity reflect on the Catholic Church while competing with it for the charity dollar.

An example of such indiscretion is a prelate in New Jersey (he will remain anonymous here) who saw a way to make a quick buck out of Pope Paul's Yankee Stadium Mass on October 4, 1965. It seems that this operator acquired the wood that had been used for the construction of the makeshift altar and the simple throne chair used by Pope Paul during that historic peace Mass. From this same wood, five-inch models of the throne chair were fashioned. The tiny wooden reconstructions were put up for sale at $17.95 apiece in an ad that used Pope Paul's name without his permission. Not surprisingly, the reproductions sold out within a week, and not long afterward more throne chairs were put up for sale—from wood that had been acquired at a nearby lumber yard.

7

IT IS A CARDINAL RULE

We have always known that heedless self-interest was bad morals; we know now that it is bad economics.—FRANKLIN D. ROOSEVELT

THE ILLUSTRIOUS FOUNDER and editor of *The New Yorker*, Harold Ross, immortalized "the little old lady in Dubuque" as not having the intellectual wherewithal to be able to appreciate his magazine. However dubious that claim may be, Dubuque has never quite lived down the observation, and the city (like Brooklyn and Oshkosh) has had to bear the brunt of being a standard one-word joke.

But Dubuque has another distinction, it too a bit farfetched. Again and again contacts in various parts of the country advised me that my book would not be complete until I had visited Dubuque. It seems that this city has a reputation—shared in part by Fall River, Massachusetts—of being run and owned by the Catholic Church, "the junior Vatican," as one individual put it.

Iowa's first permanent church, St. Raphael's, was founded at Dubuque by Dominican Samuel Mazzuchelli in 1836, and a year later the Diocese of Dubuque was established; it became an archdiocese in 1893. The Sisters of Charity of the Blessed Virgin Mary opened Clarke College for women in Dubuque in 1843, shortly after which the Brothers of St. Joseph opened an academy for boys nearby. Today the Dubuque Archdiocese has 114 elementary parochial schools, which handle over 30,000 students, and fifty-seven Catholic high schools, which have an enrollment of better than 21,000. Because the parochial schools absorb two thirds of the school-age children, the city of Dubuque has the lowest school-tax rate in the state. The three Catholic universities in the archdiocese make a significant contribution to the city's income and economic stability, according to Dubuque's city manager, who also called attention to the six Catholic convents and the two major Catholic hospitals in town.

Dubuque's population of 63,000 persons is nearly 80 percent Irish and German Catholic. Its reputation for being "a Catholic town" apparently rests on the fact that the archdiocese owns a large amount of downtown property, most of which was willed to the Church by wealthy Catholics. Other property in the upper part of the city, like the mother houses of several religious orders, the school grounds, etc., were acquired in the early days when the cost of land was low. Now these land parcels, some of which constitute the choice, scenic spots of the area, have increased considerably in value, especially since the city spread up to and around them. The archdiocese owns the city's most highly evaluated piece of property, the building on the 700 block of Main Street, which was, until recently, occupied by Montgomery Ward & Company and the F. W. Woolworth store, before they relocated in the new Kennedy Mall shopping center. Because this building provided rental income, the city of Dubuque taxed it, but other properties owned by the Church are tax exempt. The city assessor points out that there is one dollar of exempt property in the city for every three dollars of taxable property.

The city's Metropolitan Planning Commission finds that more than 40 percent of Dubuque's 62,000 developed acres are in the public or semi-public category.

As for the Catholic Church ownership of businesses in Dubuque, investigation showed that one church owned a bowling alley and that one priest privately owned a camera company, but aside from that Dubuque's reputation as a bastion of Catholic economic power seems undeserved.

Except for Rhode Island, where Roman Catholics constitute a majority of the population, Catholics are a numerical minority in every state of the Union. Though American Catholics are mainly concentrated in urban areas, the figures show that they are unevenly distributed throughout the country. Twenty-three dioceses have fewer than 50,000 Catholics, thirty-one have between 50,000 and 100,000, forty-one have between 100,000 and 250,000, eighteen have between 250,000 and 500,000, and seven have between 500,000 and a million. Seven dioceses have more than one million Catholics; these are Boston, Brooklyn, Chicago, Detroit, New York, Newark and Philadelphia. Only six dioceses—El Paso, Gallup, Mobile, Richmond, Wheeling and Wilmington—cross state lines. Geographically, the largest diocese is Reno, Nevada, with an area of 119,542 square miles, whereas the smallest diocese is Newark, New Jersey, with only 541 square miles. Every state has at least one diocese.

Let us examine the Catholic picture in each of the geographical regions of the United States.

New England (Massachusetts, Connecticut, Rhode Island, Vermont, New Hampshire and Maine). This region covers 66,608 square miles and has a Catholic population of more than 4.5 million out of a total population of nearly 12 million. It is in New England—in Rhode Island and in Fall River, Massachusetts—that one finds the only dioceses in the country in which the Catholics are a majority of the total population.

Though New England occupies a relatively small area in respect to the whole United States, its eleven dioceses make up one of the most vigorous centers of Catholic life.

Middle Atlantic States (New York, New Jersey and Pennsylvania). With a combined area of 102,745 square miles, this sector has approximately 10 million Catholics out of a total population of more than 37 million. Containing eighteen dioceses, the area has the largest single concentration of Catholics in the country.

East North-Central States (Ohio, Illinois, Indiana, Michigan and Wisconsin). More than 40 million people live in this area of 248,283 square miles, and of these more than 7.5 million are Catholics, the second largest concentration of Catholics in the country. There are twenty-six dioceses.

The South (Delaware, Georgia, Florida, Maryland, North Carolina, South Carolina, Virginia, West Virginia, Kentucky, Alabama, Mississippi, Tennessee and Washington, D.C.). Though it has an area of more than 400,000 square miles, the Catholics in the South number only about 1.6 million in a total population of more than 43 million. With fourteen dioceses, this section of America is considered the weakest in terms of Catholic numbers. There are altogether 820 counties in the U. S. that have no resident priest, and about 800 of them are in the South.

West North-Central States (Minnesota, Iowa, Missouri, North Dakota, South Dakota, Nebraska and Kansas). Covering 435,957 square miles, this portion of the United States has more than 2.3 million Catholics (out of a total population of 16 million), living in twenty-three dioceses.

West South-Central States (Arkansas, Oklahoma, Louisiana and Texas). Over 2.7 million Catholics live in this 438,883-square-mile region, which has more than 19 million inhabitants. There are twelve dioceses, but the Catholics are spread most unevenly. Of some 12 million Negroes living in the

South, 230,000 are Catholics and 148,000 of them live in Louisiana, which has the densest Catholic population. New Orleans is the site of Xavier University, the only Catholic university for blacks in America.

Mountain States (Arizona, Colorado, Idaho, Montana, Nevada, New Mexico, Utah, and Wyoming). These states, which cover 863,887 square miles, have a total population of over 8 million and a Catholic population of approximately one million.

Pacific Coast (California, Oregon, Washington, Hawaii and Alaska). This is by far the largest area of the United States, covering 916,693 square miles. The total population is nearly 27 million, of which more than 3.4 million is Roman Catholic. The states of Oregon and Washington have fewer Catholics than any other states in the country outside of the South.

Canada, with its 3.8 million square miles of territory, has a population of 20,772,000, of which 9.9 million, or 48 percent, is Roman Catholic. Nearly all of the country's Catholic citizens are located in the eastern part, and especially in the main cities like Quebec, Montreal and Toronto. In the northern and western portions of Canada, there are few Catholics to be found. The country has sixty-three dioceses, of which seventeen are archdioceses.

The basic governing unit for North America's Catholics is the archdiocese, of which there are twenty-nine in the United States. What an archdiocese is and what it is not, particularly within the frame of reference of its finances and money affairs, have never been quite clear even to practicing Roman Catholics. It is astonishing to discover just how little Catholics know about the organization of their own Church. Perhaps one priest put it best, not long ago, when he said that the role of the Catholic layman in the multimillion-dollar affairs of a given diocese is to "pray, pay and obey."

To illustrate in a general way how an archdiocese is structured and how it functions, I shall describe the Hartford Archdiocese. What applies to Roman Catholics in the state of Connecticut is in the main typical of the various jurisdictions across the land.

The Archdiocese of Hartford, like other jurisdictions throughout the United States and Canada, makes a distinction between a "diocesan priest" (of whom there are approximately 575 in the archdiocese) and a "religious priest" (of whom there are nearly 180, all members of orders). Both types show a similar disregard for personal wealth, the main difference between them being that the members of orders take a vow of poverty, while the diocesan priests do not. Defined at its most basic level, an individual who takes a vow of poverty does not receive a paycheck or accumulate possessions of value; his material needs are fully taken care of by the organization to which he is attached.

A diocesan priest, however, is on a fixed salary, according to a pay structure set down by the archdiocese. As a young curate, his weekly paycheck comes to almost $51 a week. A veteran pastor, on the other hand, receives a salary of nearly $86 a week. Some priests are allowed to keep the "extra money" they earn by the performance of certain services such as weddings, baptisms and deaths. Like anyone else, a priest must file an income-tax form and pay Internal Revenue and state taxes where applicable. In the Hartford setup a priest starts off at $220 a month and earns $240 after eight years and $260 after fifteen years. A pastor receives a paycheck of $350 per month during the first ten years and $370 thereafter. Ordinarily it takes a priest about twenty-two years to work his way up to a pastorate. Surprisingly, when a priest wins the title of monsignor, for instance, he does not receive a raise in pay, since the title is strictly honorary.

Although his room and board are paid for, a priest must buy his own clothes. His automobile is also his responsibility, as are the insurance and maintenance costs. A car can never be purchased from parish funds, but in some cases the archbishop will allow a priest to accept a car given to him by parishioners.

All diocesan priests are assigned to a parish, which are independent corporations. The officers of each parish are the bishop, a vicar general, the pastor and two laymen. But the overall chain of command is from Pope to bishop to priest. Archbishop John F. Whealon of Hartford (who, by the way, does not receive a salary but draws expenses whenever the occasion requires) is the boss of his diocese, and he answers to no one but the Pope. No other bishop, archbishop or cardinal in the United States has any kind of formal jurisdiction over Archbishop Whealon, and he has no authority over clerics outside his own archdiocese. This ought to dispel a commonly held notion that the Roman Catholic Church in the United States is one unified, consolidated entity. While it is true that there is official conformity on the religious issues and tenets which stems from Rome itself, the dioceses are self-contained and self-administered when it comes to money matters and administration.

From the chancery—a granite building on Hartford's Farmington Avenue, two doors away from the Cathedral of St. Joseph—Archbishop Whealon runs the archdiocese with the help of a staff, which includes two bishops known as vicars-general or auxiliary bishops. Carrying out policies set down by the archbishop is the executive director and business manager, a clergyman who is called the chancellor. There is also a judicial arm; its function is to rule on questions of canonical law, and it deals almost entirely with petitions to nullify marriages as a prelude to civil divorce. In addition, there are fourteen diocesan consultors, all pastors, with whom Archbishop Whealon confers when there are internal problems involving archdiocese administration, such as the removal or transferral of priests or pastors (usually for sickness or personal reasons).

Nothing of any consequence can happen in the Hartford Archdiocese's 205 parishes without the approval of the Archbishop. By sending out a pastoral letter at least once a month, Archbishop Whealon maintains a good flow of communication between the chancery and the parishes. The archdiocesan weekly newspaper, *The Catholic Transcript* (with a paid circulation of more than eighty thousand), also keeps the pastors informed. Materials from various services, which the chancery relays to pastors, also guide priests in how to deal with problems in the parochial schools, teach the catechism, implement new liturgy and take part in ecumenical activities. For general guidance the pastors depend on a book that was put together in 1959, *The First Synod of the Archdiocese of Hartford,* which lists over 320 diocesan regulations, covering clergy, laity, sacraments, worship, cemeteries, preaching, religious instructions and schools. From this book a pastor learns what the procedures are for buying a piece of land for a new church, for instance, and he learns how to undertake the business of erecting a new building.

A pastor is, for the most part, his own boss in his parish. He decides what the hours of Mass will be, organizes the Sunday school, sees that the church property is being kept in workable repair and, if there are any parochial schools in his parish, oversees their administration. He also establishes what the tuition rates for his elementary schools will be. The tuition for the diocesan high schools, however, is decided upon by Archbishop Whealon.

Helping to conduct church affairs are the laymen, whose role in recent years has enlarged, although it is mostly confined to the Catholic school system. Several years ago the Archbishop created a diocesan board of education, eleven of whose twenty members were leading Catholic laymen; these included two lawyers, two educators, a psychiatrist, a labor leader, a manufacturer, a research scientist, a dental surgeon and two housewives. In spite of the fact that the board of education does not have the power of decision, nearly all of its recommendations have been adopted by the Archbishop.

In Hartford, any layman (of any religion) can usually get a personal hearing with the Archbishop. He is known to read personally every letter sent to him, and when any of these requires further attention (of the kind that can be handled at the parish level—such as a complaint), Archbishop Whealon relays the letter to the proper priest with a request for attention, action or comment.

To run the Catholic institutions and parishes in the Hartford Archdiocese, which embraces eighty-one towns in Hartford, New Haven and Litchfield Counties, costs about $150 million each year. This sum includes budgets of $25 million for the three Catholic hospitals, up to $200,000 for each of the parochial schools, about $350,000 for each of the high schools and an average of $40,000 for the parishes. Because the archdiocese "employs" over 3,220 priests, sisters, nurses, doctors and lay teachers, it is one of Connecticut's largest employers. It also runs the largest single school system in the state—111 elementary schools, eighteen secondary schools—educating nearly 53,000 students each year.

Possessing real estate with a market value of $272 million, the Hartford Archdiocese owns more land than the state of Connecticut. Catholic holdings in the more than two hundred parishes are assessed at approximately $177.8 million. These holdings include churches and rectories in nearly all of the parishes, about 120 convents, three general hospitals, six colleges, six seminaries, ten novitiates, 129 schools and more than sixty cemeteries. The most valuable Catholic properties include St. Francis Hospital, assessed at $10.7 million; the Cathedral of St. Joseph, assessed at $7.6 million; St. Raphael Hospital in New Haven, $6 million; St. Mary Hospital in Waterbury, $5.8 million; Albertus Magnus College in New

Haven, $3 million; Mary Immaculate Academy in New Britain, $2.7 million; St. Joseph's College in West Hartford, $2.6 million; St. Thomas Seminary in Bloomfield, $2.4 million; Our Lady of Angels Academy in Enfield, $1.9 million; St. Alphonsus College in Suffield, $1.7 million; Immaculate Conception Church in Waterbury, $1.7 million; South Catholic High School in Hartford, $1.6 million; Sacred Heart Academy in Hamden, $1.4 million; La Salette Seminary in Cheshire, $1.4 million; St. Thomas Aquinas High School in New Britain, $1.3 million; Daughters of Mary of the Immaculate Conception Convent in New Britain, $1.2 million; St. Ann's Church in Waterbury, $1.2 million; Northwest Catholic High School in West Hartford, $1.2 million; Holy Family Seminary in Farmington, $1.1 million; Convent of Mary Immaculate in West Hartford, $1.1 million; Notre Dame High School in West Haven, $1.1 million; Holy Cross School in New Britain, $1 million; Sacred Heart School in New Britain, $1 million; and East Catholic High School in Manchester, $1 million.

According to official records, none of the properties is being used for nonchurch, income-producing purposes. According to attorney Joseph P. Cooney, counsel for the archdiocese, the Church owns no such real estate in the state, since "Connecticut law is strict on that."

Contrast the Hartford situation with that of another jurisdiction, the Detroit Archdiocese in Michigan. For supplying information on this jurisdiction I am indebted to Thomas J. Gumbleton, auxiliary bishop and vicar of parishes of the Detroit Archdiocese. Even though he oversees the operation, Bishop Gumbleton admits that trying to assemble the financial statements and make a comprehensive report covering all the parishes and missions (which number 360 in the Detroit Archdiocese) "would be quite a job."

"One of the things a financial report will list is buildings," declares Bishop Gumbleton. "And in terms of buildings it might look as if the Church is a very wealthy organization. Take Newman Hall [a classic-looking building used by Catholic students at Wayne State University]. That is one we are trying to unload. The building is appraised at $250,000 to $300,000. If we list that as one of our assets, you would have to say the archdiocese has a quarter of a million dollars in it." He maintains that although these buildings are expensive, they are not income-producing properties.

Another thing which causes misunderstanding in the evaluation of Catholic wealth is the failure to distinguish between property held by an archdiocese and property held by Catholic groups and Catholic individuals. Although religious orders and monasteries are Catholic, they are corporations in their own right and are not part of the archdiocese. Bishop Gumbleton makes it plain that the Knights of Columbus, for instance, owns Boysville in Clinton, Michigan, but neither Boysville nor the Knights is part of the Detroit Archdiocese. And so it is with a host of monasteries, nunneries, universities, colleges, high schools and cemeteries.

"We know what the Archbishop owns," explains Bishop Gumbleton. "He holds title in trust to all parish properties and the buildings on them and to diocesan properties. We own the sites of our parishes and missions. The sites and the buildings on them are part of our corporation. We have about thirty-five sites for future parishes—just open land with money tied up in it, and we pay taxes on it. We don't have any investments—unless you include $1,500 worth of stocks bequeathed to the Church. We have no portfolio of stocks. In fact, the archdiocese does not own income-producing property."

Bishop Gumbleton listed the major properties of the archdiocesan corporation as the Gabriel Richard Building on Michigan Avenue, the Chancery Office building on Washington Boulevard, the Catholic Charities building on Hamilton

Avenue, the Sacred Heart Seminary on West Chicago, three cemeteries, and a part of St. John's Seminary, which is owned by all five Michigan dioceses. As for the corporate worth of the archdiocese, he does not believe anybody really knows, nor is anybody, including the Archbishop, in a position to tell. Nevertheless, it can be reported that the archdiocese holds approximately $37 million on behalf of the parishes in a central loan agreement. In Detroit the parishes deposit their surplus revenues in an archdiocese-administered fund, for which they receive 3 percent interest. Of the $37 million in deposit, approximately $18 million has been borrowed back (at 5¾ percent interest) by parishes to pay creditors.

Serving as the Church's administrative headquarters for eight counties in southeastern Michigan, the Detroit Archdiocese is itself a creditor common to all of its 345 parishes. It provides a string of services, for which the parishes must pay. Such services include seminaries for training priests, social-service agencies, and administration for the whole school system. The parishes pay the archdiocese a 6 percent tax, known as the "quota." The archdiocese in turn pays a "quota" to Rome, for which no percentage or total figure has been cited; the largest amount that goes to the Vatican is from the annual Peter's Pence collection. There is no corporate financial relationship between the archdiocese and the Vatican.

Under the laws of Michigan, the Detroit Archdiocese has never had to file formal incorporation papers, as would a lay group. A law passed in 1867 empowers a Roman Catholic bishop to act as a corporation. This law, Act 207, authorizes the archbishop "to exercise without limitation . . . any and all powers relating to the temporalities of the Roman Catholic Church vested in such archbishop or bishop or administrator by virtue of his office." The act was amended in 1937, 1941 and 1954 to redefine the extent of the bishop's powers. As it stands today, John Cardinal Dearden of Detroit is limited as to his right to hold real estate; he can hold only land which is used exclusively for charitable, religious, educational, literary or burial purposes.

For the fiscal year ended June 30, 1970, the Detroit Archdiocese issued its first public report on income and expenditures. It showed that the archdiocese's income of $2,406,299 from quota payments was swelled to a total of $3,649,504 by the sale of property no longer needed for church purposes, bequests, interest, and insurance payments. Another $1,075,000 came from the Archdiocese Development Fund, bringing the total income to $4,724,504. During the year the Archdiocese Development Fund received $2,145,483, of which $1,649,232 came from contributions, $432,098 from other donations and bequests and $64,153 from interest. After $1,075,000 was used for general expenses and $1,727,731 for special commitments, there was a deficit of $657,248.

Eight diocesan collections, plus bequests and interest, brought in an additional $947,176. But since $1,032,812 was spent, there remained a deficit of $85,636. The Loan Agreement Account, in which parishes "bank" funds until they are needed, had assets of $43,042,727, after a $500,000 reserve for uncollectable accounts was set up. Of this, all but $356,194 was at work in the parishes.

The largest single outlay, $1,194,189, went to seminaries, and another large outlay, $231,874, went to the Newman Apostolate serving collegians. A grant of $215,846 was extended to the Michigan Catholic Conference, a cooperative maintained by the five dioceses in Michigan for work in the fields of education, social services, pensions and insurance. The total outlay was $4,401,376, leaving a surplus of $323,128 for the fiscal year. From an income of $191,692, the archdiocese's Clergy Health Plan paid out $189,175, leaving $2,517 to be added to the reserves. The Clergy Retirement Plan spent $319,983 of its $1,000,464 income, leaving $680,481. A total of $791,224 of that income came from a special collection taken up on Christmas.

One unusual item in the report is the salary received by the Cardinal and his two auxiliary bishops. They are paid a total of $21,750, an average of $7,250 apiece, or about $140 a week. The Cardinal and his bishops are also provided with housing and other allowances, but no amounts are specified for these.

All priests in the archdiocese receive the same basic income of $3,000 a year, plus $50 a year for each year of service and a $100-a-month transportation allowance. Detroit priests also receive room and board from the parishes they serve, plus an allowance of up to $300 a year for professional expenses that include seminars, retreats, books and newspapers. As of the beginning of 1970, priests in Detroit no longer keep the offerings given them for weddings, funerals and other Masses, but turn them over to the parish treasury. The archbishop provides all priests with Blue Cross and Blue Shield coverage for medical expenses.

The openness of the Detroit Archdiocese is to be much admired and it gives hope that perhaps other archdioceses may one day offer their parishioners a look into their inner operations. How long this may take in some instances is difficult to predict, for the degree of sensitivity regarding archdiocesan internal matters, especially those dealing with funds, seems to be in direct proportion to the degree of insensitivity a given archbishop might have toward his people. James Francis Cardinal McIntyre, Archbishop of Los Angeles until 1970, is a case in point. The Cardinal, known among his fellow bishops as a reactionary, was not one to tolerate inquiries about the money of his archdiocese. Once when veteran newspaperman Robert B. Kaiser, a former Vatican correspondent for *Time* magazine, attempted to ask him questions about archdiocesan funds, Cardinal McIntyre suddenly asked him to leave. Mr. Kaiser reported the incident in an article in *West*, the Los Angeles *Times* Sunday magazine, and it raised the curiosity of the *Times*'s editors, who subsequently assigned a reporter to do a story on church properties in Los Angeles. Fully researched and written, the story was set and ready for the press, but at the last minute an order came down from the publisher's office to kill it. Some say it was because the story tweaked hierarchical sensitivities.

Before he retired in 1970, Cardinal McIntyre did make some financial disclosures, however. Because California law requires that taxes be paid on church property and other structures not strictly religious in function, the Los Angeles Archdiocese had to pay more than $1.6 million in levies. The breakdown showed assessments of $316,136 paid on elementary and high schools, convents, halls and auditoriums; a total of $727,002 paid by the more than 310 parishes for assessments on church buildings and for taxes on rectories and "other parish properties"; taxes and assessments paid by the archdiocese on land for future parish and school sites and other non-tax-exempt property.

By the time of his retirement at the age of eighty-three, Cardinal McIntyre—who had been a successful and wealthy stockbroker before entering the priesthood at twenty-nine—had won acclaim as a builder of churches and schools. His building program had started almost immediately following his appointment as archbishop in 1948. During Los Angeles' postwar population boom, 110 churches and schools were built under his aegis.

One plan of Cardinal McIntyre's that never quite materialized, however, was the construction of a huge development. The archdiocese had acquired a large parcel of land fronting on Wilshire Boulevard and planned to put up a twenty-story hotel, a twenty-two-story office building, two large apartment buildings and a single-story office building, to stretch for three blocks along the boulevard. The buildings were to occupy only 26 percent of the land, so that the central area could have tennis courts, a swimming pool and a parklike setting. There were to have been three underground levels, with parking space for 3,400 automobiles. Opposition to the plan grew from owners of 114 lots surrounding the property, who argued that commercial use of the church-owned block would depreciate the value of their homes. Late in 1962 Archbishop McIntyre won his suit to have the undeveloped block removed from restrictions limiting construction to residences, but at the time of this writing the block on Wilshire Boulevard was still an empty lot. A paved parking area had been made out of a section of it, however, and the Sisters of the Sacred Heart were using the only house on the property as a residence when I inspected it. Archbishop Timothy Manning, who succeeded Cardinal McIntyre, would give no explanation of why the building plans were not carried through, but knowledgeable sources indicated that problems had developed in the financing as a result of the increasing drain that parochial schools had been making on archdiocesan resources.

Cardinal McIntyre's "building mania" was matched by that of Francis Cardinal Spellman, Archbishop of New York, a man with similar ideas and values and an equally thorough knowledge of business and economics. Cardinal Spellman, however, left his mark not only on his archdiocese but on all American Catholicism.

When Spellman was appointed to head the New York Archdiocese, he found it burdened with a debt of more than $28 million. Immediately he put into play a talent that almost amounted to genius. Working closely with bankers and corporation executives, he undertook a policy of reorganization, of which an aggressive building program was no small part. With an annual outlay of about $50 million, the New York Archdiocese became the scene of a construction program that made Spellman the biggest builder in New York, second only to the city of New York itself. The money was spent to build churches, hospitals, convents, schools, seminaries and homes for the aged.

One financial expert who collaborated with New York's Archbishop said in describing him, "There's nothing abstract about the Cardinal. He tells you exactly what he wants and then lets you do it." Perhaps more illustrative of the Cardinal's special talents is an anecdote once printed by *Fortune* magazine. Actually it is a story that was stolen from behind the Vatican walls and modified by the magazine. According to the *Fortune* version, "Spelly" (an affectionate nickname that both clergy and laity who knew him personally used) presented himself at the gates of heaven, where he was asked by Saint Peter for his name and a few facts about himself that might be considered in his favor. "My name is Francis Cardinal Spellman," he announced, "but I prefer to think of myself as a simple parish priest who had nearly two million souls." Explaining that he would have to check into the official files, Saint Peter went off, but when he came back he said he was sorry but he had not been able to find a dossier on Spellman, Francis. "Perhaps," he suggested, "Your Eminence's good works have been listed under another category?" A bit disappointed, the Cardinal said that he had published prayers, poems, meditations and even a novel. Once again Saint Peter went off, and once again he came back empty-handed. "I'm afraid, sir, that your writings, however commendable, have not been included in our files. Is there something else, some other activity, that could have attracted our attention?" Reluctantly, the Cardinal pointed out that he had, among other things, built fifty churches and two hundred schools, as well as hospitals, homes for the aged and other charitable establishments too numerous to count. So for the third time Saint Peter went off, but this time he came back with a beaming smile. "Come right in, Frank," he said apologetically. "We had you under 'Real Estate.' "

From his brownstone chancery behind St. Patrick's Cathedral Cardinal Spellman directed the operations of the richest archdiocese in the world. His administrative apparatus radiated, as it still does under his successor, Terence Cardinal Cooke, from a four-story mansion on Madison Avenue between Fiftieth and Fifty-first Streets. Long known as the Powerhouse, this Italian Renaissance building served as Cardinal Spellman's headquarters from 1939 to the day he died, in December 1967. In his first sermon from the pulpit of St. Patrick's, he told the parishioners that he was not overly impressed by New York's reputation as the richest archdiocese in the Catholic world. Recognizing that a debt of $28 million would take a long time to overcome, he forthwith began to make friends with every important New York businessman, Gentile and non-Gentile. He instituted a practice of staging regular luncheons or dinners for bankers, financiers, real-estate men, Wall Street brokers, business editors, corporation executives, labor leaders and other solid personalities in the world of business and commerce.

It paid off. The charming and affable clergyman not only made a vast number of influential personal friends but derived considerable information about big business. His assimilation of the knowledge he received from these individuals is borne out by his twenty-eight-year record as head of the archdiocese. These friends, each of whom was a specialist in his own field, formed part of a circle of trusted lay advisers. For instance, the Cardinal drew heavily on the suggestions and advice offered him by an influential New York financial editor, an expert on the stock market. Others in the Spellman advisory stable included John Reynolds, a real-estate broker;

Charles Silver, a businessman noted for his civic and philanthropic activities; and John A. Coleman, a Wall Street broker. Mr. Coleman, who began his Wall Street career over a half century ago and who is head of Adler, Coleman & Company, is known as "the Pope of Wall Street." It was, in fact, John Coleman who was the first man to greet and shake hands with Pope Paul VI at Kennedy Airport on the occasion of his unprecedented trip to New York City. Several years ago, when the Vatican had $30 million it wanted to invest in the New York stock market, Cardinal Spellman asked Mr. Coleman to handle the portfolio for the Pontiff—which he did, by investing most of the money in Boeing, Lockheed, National Steel, Douglas and Curtiss-Wright stocks.

One of the first things that the Cardinal gleaned from his new friends was the information that the archdiocese could borrow money at 2 percent repayable in five years or at $2\frac{1}{3}$ percent repayable in ten years, whereas the various parishes, being smaller, had to pay 5 and 6 percent on loans. By creating an archdiocesan bank, Cardinal Spellman saved the Catholic Church about a half-million dollars a year; the parishes would no longer borrow directly from a regular bank but from the central Spellman bank created with money he had borrowed at the lower interest rates.

He applied a similar principle to acquisitions. Recognizing that he would have the advantage of discounts if he bought supplies such as candles in large lots, he set up a system whereby the archdiocese would do all the buying for the parishes. Thus the archdiocese business office, which today employs over fifty persons, buys everything from wine for Masses to parish automobiles (six thousand a year), bringing the total saving to approximately $1 million a year on total expenditures of $14 million. Now more than twenty such central purchasing offices, patterned after the Spellman type, have been opened by various dioceses in the United States and Canada to take advantage of low costs through bulk purchasing.

After centralizing purchases and creating an archdiocese bank, "the Boss" (to give him the nickname by which he was universally known among his close colleagues within the archdiocese) ordered the curtailing of parish fiscal autonomy, centralized and refinanced the debt, consolidated insurance coverage and established firm controls on spending and building.

It was shortly after the end of the Second World War, when the building industry in New York City, after a long layoff, was champing at the bit to get started, that Cardinal Spellman made his move into construction. At a dinner at the Hotel Astor where he addressed a gathering of construction company presidents and labor leaders, he described the building program that the archdiocese wanted to put into operation. He said he stood ready to throw $25 million worth of work to those companies which would give him a reasonable cost estimate. The speech had impact. Within a few days a number of contracts had been signed, and the archdiocese now embarked on building projects that were to continue throughout his administration.

Among the late Cardinal's notable real-estate accomplishments are the $5-million Archbishop Stepinac High School in White Plains, the $6-million Cardinal Spellman High School in the Bronx, and the $11-million Foundling Hospital on New York's Lexington Avenue. The construction that took place during Cardinal Spellman's tenure has been valued at better than $400 million—a record that few other churchmen can match.

Another example of the Cardinal's business perspicacity was his handling of a piece of property on Madison Avenue between Eighty-first and Eighty-second Streets. The land had been leased by the city of New York in 1866 to Archbishop

John McCloskey for ninety-nine years at an annual rental of one dollar. The stipulation had been that the property was to be used by the Sisters of Mercy for an industrial school. In 1944 Cardinal Spellman purchased it from New York for the sum of $275,000, and six years later the city bought the property back for $1,350,000—or $1,075,000 more than the price paid by Cardinal Spellman.

Always a controversial figure, largely because of his political activities—most of which were based on his strong anti-Communist feelings—Cardinal Spellman was never namby-pamby when it concerned the dollars and cents of his archdiocese. In 1948, for instance, he made national headlines and was called a scab by union leaders when he broke a strike of 240 members of the United Cemetery Workers Union, C.I.O., against Calvary Cemetery in Queens for a five-day week and a basic wage of $77.23. While the gravediggers, all of whom were Roman Catholics, picketed the burial ground and the chancery, Cardinal Spellman led several dozen divinity students from St. Joseph's Seminary in Yonkers through the picket lines to dig graves for the one thousand coffins that had accumulated. Eventually the strikers joined an A.F.L. union, and the Cardinal approved a contract for an 8.3 percent raise over the pre-strike wage of $59.40. To help make up the money lost by the strikers' families, Cardinal Spellman had covering checks sent out to them. Looking back on his strike-breaking role, he admitted to newspapermen that it had confronted him with "one of the most difficult, grievous, heartbreaking issues that has ever come within my time as Archbishop of New York."

Nor was Cardinal Spellman namby-pamby when it came to playing political cards and laying his aces on the table. In January 1966, several days after John V. Lindsay had been sworn in as mayor of New York City, Cardinal Spellman paid him a call. After the usual formalities, he dropped a sheet of paper on the new mayor's desk and bluntly told him, "That's our list of jobs." This list was made up of Catholics whom the Cardinal was personally recommending for appointive positions in the city government—judgeships, school administrative posts and places in the real-estate division. Rather than invite open warfare with the New York Archbishop, the New York mayor complied with many of the suggestions, at least enough to keep him quiet. One of the men on that roster (now deceased) was given the position of building superintendent of New York City's school system (despite the fact that he did not have the qualification of a degree in engineering), a post that involved the awarding of millions of dollars in public-school construction contracts to building companies. Every construction-firm president knew that Cardinal Spellman was 100 percent behind this man and that any time the archdiocese invited bids for building a Catholic school it was good business to pare the cost estimates to the very bone or even offer out-and-out discounts to the Cardinal. It is not known how many millions of dollars Cardinal Spellman saved with this kind of subtle intimidation.

Sometimes the Cardinal could be heavyhanded. For instance, Pope Paul VI once took off his tiara in a ceremony at St. Peter's Basilica in Rome and placed it on the altar, saying that the tiara was to be a gift to the millions of poor people throughout the world, but somehow it ended up as a possession of Cardinal Spellman, a collector of ecclesiastical souvenirs. A syndicated Catholic columnist, John Leo, took exception to this. He reported that the tiara had been brought out during a testimonial dinner at the Waldorf-Astoria and displayed as the latest acquisition in the Cardinal's collection. If anybody had forgotten about the Pope's having offered it to the poor, the Leo column reminded thousands of readers, some of whom, though admirers of Cardinal Spellman, registered strong objection. The fuss did not seem to bother Cardinal Spellman. The tiara is now on permanent display at the National Shrine of the Immaculate Conception in Washington, D.C.

Pope Paul had a difficult choice in selecting a successor to Cardinal Spellman. At the chancery, the Cardinal had had two administrative assistants—Bishop John J. Maguire and Bishop Terence J. Cooke. Bishop Maguire, in his sixties, was a specialist in personnel problems, while Bishop Cooke, in his late forties, had had the responsibility of overseeing archdiocesan finances. Though it had been expected that Bishop Maguire would succeed to the post, the Pope decided on the younger man, the one with the financial expertise—apparently on Spellman's own strong personal recommendation. Cardinal Cooke, now in his early fifties, may have come to his post as a "Spelly man," but he has developed a "style" of his own, although much of the Spellman business activity continues in the way the late Cardinal would have desired.

Contrary to what some people assume, the New York Archdiocese does not include all of New York City. There is a separate jurisdiction called the Brooklyn Archdiocese, which includes the counties of Kings (Brooklyn), Queens, Nassau and Suffolk. The New York Archdiocese, second only to the Chicago Archdiocese in terms of population, embraces ten counties, which include New York (Manhattan), Bronx, Richmond (Staten Island), Westchester, Putnam, Rockland, Orange, Sullivan, Ulster and Dutchess. Within its jurisdiction are more than 2,200 priests, nearly 10,000 nuns and brothers, 408 parishes, 332 elementary schools, 98 high schools (with more than 215,000 students and 7,800 teachers), 21 colleges and universities and 41 hospitals, old-age homes and orphanages.

Like every other archdiocese in the United States and Canada, Cardinal Cooke's domain is property rich and cash poor. Facing a financial squeeze, the archdiocese—which under the

1939–1967 Spellman reign accounted for nearly a half billion dollars' worth of new construction—has about $150 million in various building and renovation projects. In recent years, a cutback was ordered on new school construction. This decision has come about as a result of the moving away from New York City of affluent Catholic groups such as Irish, Italians and Germans and the influx of poor Spanish-speaking people and of poor blacks from the South.

The effect these population moves has had on the archdiocese has become quite visible. Take, for instance, the St. Angela Merici Parish in the Bronx, which in the early 1960s, with a congregation that was predominantly white and middle-class, undertook a $700,000 building program for a school extension and a new convent. A total of $400,000 was quite easily raised, and the balance was borrowed. At the present time, more than half of the parishioners are Puerto Ricans, Cubans or blacks, and the church is having difficulty meeting the quarterly debt payments of $5,000.

That the raising of money in the New York Archdiocese has become a big problem today is borne out by the reluctance of Cardinal Cooke to engage in major fund-raising drives. The last two drives showed the trend. In 1960 the chancery raised $37 million cash and pledges in order to build high schools and seminaries. Four years later, on the twenty-fifth anniversary of Cardinal Spellman's appointment as archbishop, a quota of only $15 million was set, yet the drive fell far short of the figure.

Until its investments on the New York Stock Exchange stopped doing well, the archdiocese managed to put its profits into new investments. Today all such earnings go into the archdiocese's current expenses, which are higher than at any time in its history. In December 1966, when the archdiocese sold approximately $25.5 million worth of Listerine royalty rights, much of the profit had to go into meeting operating expenses. What has hurt the archdiocese most—and this applies throughout the United States and Canada—is the exodus of middle-class Catholics and the defection of individuals who do not see eye to eye with church officialdom on some controversial social issues like birth control, celibacy and divorce. Meanwhile, the parochial-school systems have become increasingly expensive. The archdiocesan high schools alone have a deficit of $2.5 million each year, and by the end of 1972, the Committee on Catholic Education says, the parochial-school system will have an estimated cash deficit of $30 million. Moreover, the number of teaching nuns has been declining steadily, and the archdiocese has had to find lay teachers to fill the vacancies.

It costs the New York Archdiocese up to $6,500 a year more to hire a lay teacher to replace a nun. As a result of the cost increases in the parochial schools, more than a hundred of the 408 parishes can no longer support themselves. Many others operate at the breaking point, and it appears that it won't be long before better than half of the 408 will be in the red each year. Grappling with the urgent problems of the parochial-school system, and the problem of Catholic education in New York, Cardinal Cooke faces a particularly ticklish situation in that he will eventually have to double the amount of money being put into the existing schools or cut back on the number of schools. In the final analysis, if the people of New York show evidence that they no longer want Catholic schools, then officials of the archdiocese are ready to undertake a plan whereby most of the parochial schools will be phased out over a ten-year period.

New York's fund-raising problems might have benefited from the skills of Boston's former Cardinal Archbishop. Nobody in the history of the American Catholic Church, not even Cardinal Spellman, could match the fund-raising record of the late Richard Cardinal Cushing. It has been estimated that when that earthy septuagenarian prelate retired in 1970, he had raised during his twenty-six years in office more than $350 million—which breaks down to $37,000 a day, or roughly $25 a minute. The Boston *Globe* cited the following incident as an illustration of the Cushing know-how: In 1962, a few days before Christmas, Attorney General Robert F. Kennedy telephoned Cardinal Cushing and asked him if he could raise a million dollars within twenty-four hours. Mr. Kennedy's request came because he needed $2.9 million in ransom money to free veterans of the Bay of Pigs invasion from Cuban jails. The Cardinal, a long-time confidant and adviser to the Kennedy family, replied, "I'll call you back in three hours, Bobby." And he did. By six o'clock that evening the Boston prelate had borrowed the funds from Latin-American friends in New England and was able to inform Mr. Kennedy that the money would be delivered that same day.

Cardinal Cushing was not to be bested in fund raising. When he needed money to relieve his debt-ridden parishes and charitable facilities, he was quick to point out that in recent drives Chicago's Catholics had raised $43 million, New York's $39 million and Brooklyn's $38 million. Therefore, he said, if Boston wanted to go into first place, Boston should kick in at least $50 million. Boston did.

Yet in spite of all the money he raised, he left the Boston Archdiocese heavily in the red. At last appraisal Boston was about $55 million in debt—largely because the archdiocese supports six hospitals (which have a total of 1,650 beds), four convalescent homes, facilities for the aged, 342 parochial schools and 56 private schools; the hospitals and convalescent homes serve more than 270,000 general patients and more than 17,000 special patients every year. Although charges were never leveled at Cardinal Cushing for mismanagement, his most ardent admirers and friends were aware of the man's limitations and often took a dim view of the "loose manner" in which he parceled out lump sums of money to his vast network of charities.

Cardinal Cushing's venture into the business world could not match that of his onetime counterpart in New York, Cardinal Spellman. The Boston Cardinal was no businessman. For years he owned a number of shares of American Telephone & Telegraph on the New York market, and though he frequently transacted these shares in a speculative manner, he never quite derived any appreciable revenue from this activity; he just could not learn the ropes.

On the other hand, the Boston Archdiocese is a big landlord, second only to the government in the amount of real estate it owns in Boston. Since these landholdings do not produce revenue, they are classified as tax free. Boston has the highest percentage of untaxed property in the nation, more than 47 percent—with a total valuation of more than $1.2 billion as of the end of 1969. The tax-exempt property in the control of the Boston Archdiocese, representing 61.2 percent of the total religious property, comes to a total of $92.7 million in assessed valuation, according to Emmett Kelley, a district director in the Boston assessor's office. It takes twenty pages to list the properties of the Boston Archdiocese in the *Official Catholic Directory*. One of these properties, Boston College, with an enrollment of more than twelve thousand students, is worth close to $65 million. The archdiocese's schools, academies, seminaries, convents, monasteries and other educational institutions are assessed at $36 million. Emmanuel College, for instance, is assessed at $8.6 million, the Christian Brothers School at $1.2 million and Boston College High School at $5.3 million. The following are also identified on the tax rolls: Carney Hospital, $6.6 million; St. Elizabeth Hospital, $6.1 million; the Home for Catholic Children, $2.7 million; Franciscan Missionaries, $2 million; Carmelite Sisters, $1 million; Bernardine Sisters, $750,000; Salesian Society, $656,200; and a number of others.

Cardinal Cushing presided over this empire in his own expansive way. For he was the kind of man who spent money like water. There was, for instance, the time he wanted a theater in which to show religious motion pictures and purchased, in 1959, the largest movie house in New England, the Loew's State Theatre, which had a seating capacity of 3,580. Assessed at $1.14 million, the theater property also included seventeen small offices. The Boston Archdiocese held on to the showplace (renamed the Donnelly Memorial Theatre) for four years, using it for film presentations and stage productions, before unloading it to the Christian Science Church for an undisclosed price. The theater has since been razed and in its place is a parking lot.

This characteristic of not knowing how to handle money, spiced with his idiosyncratic surges of generosity, gave Cardinal Cushing a "regular-guy" image with the people who worked under his wing, irrespective of what it may have done to the archdiocese's bank balance. For instance, whenever the Boston cardinal had occasion to visit in the parishes, he invariably handed out money or gifts of one kind or another. As was his wont, following coffee and cookies in the dining room of a convent, he would ask the nuns, "Sisters, is there something you may be needing now?" Even when the mother superior would shake her head and say she needed nothing, Cardinal Cushing was not taking this kind of No for an answer. "Well," he would say with a knowing nod of his head, "I think you girls could use a new refrigerator." If it was not a refrigerator, then it would be a sewing machine, or a record-player, or a washing machine, or some-such. Then he would turn to one of his associates and bark, "Monsignor, find some loose change and buy our girls what they need before the week is out!"

A short while after his retirement, Cardinal Cushing died, and his will, filed for probate several months later, contained the following sentence: "I entered the service of God poor and without property. I have always aspired to leave it equally unencumbered. I have no insurance, bank deposits, investments, nor any other holdings whatsoever."

Yet, in spite of some mistakes, Cardinal Cushing was a chip off the papal block and a special favorite of Pope John XXIII. No doubt this was because they were kindred spirits in that neither was awed by precedent and both were profoundly human. When Pope John died, he left to the craggy, erect Cushing one of the two pectoral crosses he had worn during his papacy. Characteristically, Cardinal Cushing gave the cross as a gift to a group of nuns. The lantern-jawed prelate, whose quick wit and delivery became a kind of trademark, said of Pope John, "John was the only man who ever understood me—and that's something, because I don't understand myself."

Such quips were a regular thing with the Cardinal, particularly during the public addresses he made to raise money. Once when a fire broke out in the wiring of a loudspeaker and smoke wafted from the lectern, the familiar gravel voice filled the auditorium, growling, "I guess it's the Devil asking for equal time."

8

THE PATER PRINCIPLE:
LIFE WITH FATHER

The religion that sets men to rebel and fight against their government . . . is not the sort of religion upon which people can go to heaven.—ABRAHAM LINCOLN

IN SAN FRANCISCO several years ago, after St. Mary's Cathedral was razed by a fire, the archdiocese quickly announced a fund-raising campaign for its rebuilding. Although the public, both Catholic and non-Catholic, was to contribute the money for a new church, chancery officials did not consult community leaders about plans for the new cathedral and as it turned out their choice of design was embarrassingly poor. The Catholic Art Forum took serious exception to the plans, but San Francisco's diocesan newspaper ignored the group's protests and refused to give space to its critical comments, meanwhile continuing to give considerable favorable attention to the Archbishop's design. Frustrated, the Art Forum brought its case to the San Francisco *Chronicle*. The downtown daily assigned its art critic to the story, and he took up the cudgels for a cathedral that would be more in keeping with established levels of art. The pressure brought to bear on Archbishop Joseph Mc-

Gucken by the daily newspaper had its results, for he changed not only his architects but also the plans. Now San Francisco was assured of having a cathedral of acceptable artistic merit.

Most church officials expect Catholic newspapers, particularly their own local weeklies, to represent them and their activities in a flattering light. The Catholic press in the United States today, with some notable exceptions, of course, does not generally offer its readers any kind of opinion that differs from that of the bishop. Official diocesan newspapers are largely used as tools. Most editors of Catholic papers are "kept men" who avoid printing news items that would be embarrassing to or critical of the Church; the Catholic press in general seeks to please the ecclesiastical piper who calls the tune. Perhaps the situation was best described by Professor Edward A. Walsh, head of the journalism department at Fordham University and the chief judge at the annual magazine competition of the Catholic Press Association, when he said, "We have far too few Catholic publications of distinction; we have far too many that are, or ought to be, candidates for extinction."

In the United States today there are approximately 150 Catholic weeklies and nearly 410 Catholic magazines. Cumulatively, they have a total readership of about 28 million, or one out of every eight Americans. In spite of the fact that more than $50 million a year in advertising is placed in these publications, nearly all of them operate at a loss—which has to be underwritten either by a local bishop or by a Catholic order or organization sponsoring a given publication.

However great the annual loss, the local bishop wants a newspaper published in his area because he believes it gives him a direct line of communication to his people. Apparently indifferent to editorial excellence, bishops tend to look upon "their" newspaper as a means of manipulating Catholic public opinion to their advantage. This is why bishops are reluctant to allow any dissenting opinion; this is why diocesan newspapers usually do not carry news that is considered unfavorable to a bishop's point of view. No officer who has poured money into a newspaper wants that newspaper to challenge his official authority. Is it any wonder, therefore, that most Catholic newspapers do not have a letters-to-the-editor column? When such a feature does appear, all letters are prudently screened by a clerical eye.

The Catholic newspapers nevertheless are growing in circulation and today sell about six million copies a week—more than double the number sold a quarter of a century ago. For newspapers generally, increased circulation is no assurance of prosperity, since the cost of distributing them, whether by subscription or by vendors, is so high. Catholic newspapers, however, are protected against the dangers of the open market by parochial-school circulation drives and other gimmicks involving quotas for each parish in a diocese. The first issue (May 1962) of *The Long Island Catholic*, for example, had an automatic circulation of 208,000, with an extremely low distribution cost.

One of the most conservative of the Catholic newspapers is *The Twin Circle* of Culver City, California. This 105,000-circulation weekly is a subsidiary of the Schick Investment Corporation, owned by West Coast industrialist Patrick J. Frawley. During the summer of 1970 *The Twin Circle* purchased *The National Register*, a moderate Catholic weekly in Denver, Colorado, with a paid circulation of 110,000, which also publishes paperback books and produces daily radio programs in 610 cities and television shows in forty-two cities. (The purchase of *The National Register* did not include the twenty-four regional and diocesan editions of the Register System of Newspapers—published at the *Register*'s Denver printing plant). Because *The Twin Circle* fights alleged departures from orthodox Catholicism, there was opposition by thirty of Denver's priests and by the 200-member Catholics for a Better Society. The Denver group said that it wanted a moderate newspaper that expressed a balanced and fair view of Catholic issues, and that *The National Register* would become too conservative under the new ownership.

It would be unfair, of course, to lump together all Catholic publications, for there are several notable diocesan newspapers which show an uninhibited handling of news. Foremost among these are *The Virginian Catholic, The Oklahoma City Courier, The Baton Rouge Catholic Commentator, The Indianapolis Criterion, The Boston Pilot, The Pittsburgh Catholic,* and the *National Catholic Reporter*. The last-named paper, which was founded as an independent Catholic publication in 1964 and which is published in Kansas City, Missouri, is an aggressively liberal weekly that enjoys an enviable record of scoops. It created a worldwide sensation in the winter of 1967 when it printed the secret majority report of the Pope's birth-control commission, which called for Vatican approval of contraception, a recommendation that was ignored by Pope Paul in his "Humanae Vitae" encyclical. The story was picked up by all the wire agencies and almost every newspaper—but not by the National Catholic News Service, which, with 150 foreign correspondents and 120 domestic correspondents, serves more than 550 publications and radio stations in sixty-five countries. Nor did the Catholic news agency do any kind of follow-up on the majority report, a fact that angered some of its clients.

No one could have been more annoyed with the *National Catholic Reporter* than Bishop Paul Tanner, who was the general overseer of the National Catholic News Service, and Egidio Cardinal Vagnozzi, the Apostolic Delegate in Washington, who firmly believed that the Catholic press should be kept under tight control lest it spread any "erroneous ideas and dangerous opinions." Whether pressure from them and other manifestations of official displeasure have been responsible for the *N.C.R.*'s recent loss of 22 percent of its circulation cannot be accurately determined. But the rebel Kansas City newspaper continues to make money—and continues to publish news stories that no other church publication will consider, to keep its letters column open to public views on controversial issues, and to stress the accountability of church officers who often think they should answer to no one. For these reasons, it is often said that the paper's editor, Robert Hoyt, is perhaps the most feared Catholic layman in the United States.

Sharing some of the spotlight with Mr. Hoyt are the editors of a number of Catholic magazines that compare favorably with their secular counterparts. These include such magazines as *America*, a weekly journal of opinion; *The Sign*, an open-minded monthly; *Cross Currents*, a high-powered intellectual journal; and *Commonweal*, a crusading weekly. The last-named magazine printed an account by an *N.C.R.* staff writer of the behind-the-scenes attempts to suppress the story of the official displeasure over *N.C.R.*'s publication of the Pope's secret commission report.

No discussion of the Catholic press would be complete without mention of the *Catholic Digest*, a phenomenon even by lay standards. In 1936 a priest in St. Paul, Minnesota, armed with a large basket of address labels and $1,000 in cash, went against the advice of all his superiors and brought out a magazine that was an unabashed imitator of *Reader's Digest*. This new *Catholic Digest* had an initial press run of thirteen thousand, half of which went out as complimentary copies. A year later, although *Catholic Digest* had intruded with virtually no capital into a risky field, its circulation had risen to 25,000 paid subscribers, and the magazine had begun making a profit even without any advertising revenue.

Amateurish and dull though those first issues were, *Catholic Digest* nevertheless continued to grow in circulation and in size. From a modest sixty-four pages of solid type on gray paper, the *Digest* fattened within a few years to ninety-six pages of better-quality paper enlivened with artwork that eventually included color. It also began to attract name writers like Rex Beach, John La Farge, Hilaire Belloc, Barbara Ward and Fulton J. Sheen. In time the magazine also gave birth to a monthly book club that attracted 56,000 members and to two other specialized slick-paper publications aimed at "the 3-billion- to 4-billion-dollar Catholic trade market." A Braille edition of the *Digest*, introduced in 1940, was published for sixteen years, until costs became so prohibitive that it had to be suspended. Editions of *Catholic Digest* appeared in French, German, Spanish and Italian, not to mention the English-language editions for Ireland and the Philippines.

In April 1954, when the *Digest's* circulation had reached almost a million, advertising began to appear on its pages. During its first year of soliciting ads, the magazine sold fifty-five pages of advertising, most of the insertions being inside and back-cover displays offering missals and Catholic insurance plans. As the rates went up from $1,312 to $1,500 a full page, the products changed. Cigarette and liquor ads were accepted, as were insertions for hearing aids, Canadian travel and the *Encyclopaedia Britannica*. It ranked seventy-eighth among all periodicals in the number of advertising pages, and eightieth in advertising-dollar revenue in 1963.

Catholic Digest became the most successful Catholic magazine in all history—and perhaps the most influential publication in the Catholic world. When its twenty-fifth anniversary edition came out in 1961—with a record 144 pages, a size that remained for subsequent numbers—the priest-owned corporation that published the magazine grossed better than $5 million. The number of copies being sold had reached a guaranteed Audit Bureau of Circulation figure of 650,000.

Despite the phenomenal success of *Catholic Digest*, it was hit—like every other newspaper and magazine—with rising costs of production and distribution. Its troubles began to build up, though it remained, circulationwise, the largest of any religious periodical in the United States. In 1964, in a move to legally avoid the payment of taxes, the owners of the *Digest* made a gift of it, together with its related publishing enterprises, to the College of St. Thomas in St. Paul. By agreement, the Reverend Paul Bussard stayed on as publisher, and the editorial and business staffs also remained intact. Financially, however, the *Digest*'s fortunes continued to dip, as did its circulation. A few years ago, as the magazine's losses mounted, the College of St. Thomas made plans to remove Father Bussard as the *Digest* publisher, but he took his case to court and won a restraining order enjoining the college from forcing him into retirement.

Publications like *Catholic Digest*, which almost never printed anything offensive to the hierarchy, were cogs in the Catholic power structure in the United States. Though the *Digest* never became an "official" publication, it was always well received by the Catholic power trust in Washington, especially the National Catholic Welfare Conference. The N.C.W.C., with a staff of more than two hundred workers, represents some 220 organized bishops of the United States. Based on Massachusetts Avenue, not far from the White House, it is the nerve center of American Catholicism.

The offices of the N.C.W.C. are busy with young priests, pamphleteers, newspapermen and lawyers who keep the Catholic population of America informed on "Catholic issues" as they arise. Its staff sends out about 75,000 words every week in news releases and editorial articles to the country's 150 Catholic newspapers—one reason why the first pages of America's diocesan papers so often resemble each other.

Curiously, the N.C.W.C. once came exceedingly close to being dissolved. Following the death of Pope Benedict XV in 1922, it was learned that he had signed an order decreeing the end of the organization. Although his successor, Pope Pius XI, had every intention of promulgating the decree, political pressures within the Church were brought to bear. Pope Pius decided to save the N.C.W.C. To cover up, it was leaked out that "some enemies of Americanism" had sneaked a forged sheet of paper onto the late Pope's desk after his death. But in allowing the N.C.W.C. to go on, Pope Pius made it known to his clergy that the organization was an arm of the hierarchy and not of the American Catholic people.

The N.C.W.C. speaks with one voice. Thus, when it talks about tax appropriations for private schools or against the recognition of Red China, every legislator knows what the "Catholic position" is. By and large, the N.C.W.C. rarely makes a direct statement *per se*, but it manages to convey the "Catholic position" on a given issue mostly through its news service and the Catholic newspapers across the country.

At one time the N.C.W.C. maintained a paid lobbyist on Capitol Hill, but today the organization does not feel such a need even though it continues, in its own way, to clutch at Washington's coattails. Catholic lobbying can be described as indirect. It could take the form of a press interview with a leading archbishop in another part of the country. When, for example, Cardinal Spellman was still alive, an interview or statement from him would alert politicians everywhere as to how far they could extend themselves without "offending" the so-called Catholic vote. It could also take the form of simultaneous sermons from various Sunday pulpits, which would give the members of Congress and the state legislatures their cue. Hence, a registered lobbyist for the N.C.W.C. would almost be superfluous, since the organization is quite able to guide Congressmen without specific directives on individual bills. Small wonder, then, that bishops or priests rarely appear at Congressional committee hearings.

Yet, despite the absence of a paid, full-time resident lobbyist in the nation's capital, the Catholic Church runs what is certainly the most powerful religious pressure group in Washington. One can go on and on, detailing the various campaigns in which the Church agitated for its special interests. I will mention only two here.

An arm of the Catholic lobby, guided by Cardinal Spellman during the mid-'50s, contributed heavily to the United States' early involvement in Vietnam in support of Ngo Dinh Diem, the Catholic President of South Vietnam. A former student at Maryknoll, the Catholic seminary outside New York City, Mr. Diem was a personal friend of Cardinal Spellman, and it caused no excitement, therefore, when the New York Archbishop flew to Saigon during the Christmas holidays in 1954 to present the Diem regime a check for $100,000 from Catholic Relief. No sooner had he come back than Cardinal Spellman enlisted the support of then Vice-President Nixon for U.S. financial aid to South Vietnam as well as for military advisers. Eventually, a reluctant President Eisenhower bowed to the Spellman urgings and the Nixon counsel and sent about a thousand American military advisers to Saigon. To shore up Mr. Diem's Catholic rule in a country with a population that was better than three-quarters Buddhist, Cardinal Spellman hired a public-relations man who helped organize a militant group called the American Friends of Vietnam. Monsignor Robert C. Hartnett, an editor of the Jesuit magazine *America*, served as one of the organization's directors. It should be noted in passing that Cardinal Spellman remained a hawk about the Vietnam War until the day he died. His herculean behind-the-scenes lobbying was instrumental in getting the White House to increase the American commitment to thirty thousand military in 1961, but no one suspected that the time would come when President Lyndon B. Johnson would escalate the war into a major conflagration.

Cardinal Spellman's lobbying derived some of its strength

from adherents in Congress—House Speaker John W. Mc-Cormack of Massachusetts, Senator Thomas J. Dodd of Connecticut, Senator John O. Pastore of Rhode Island, Congressmen John J. Rooney and Eugene Keogh of Brooklyn, and Congressman James J. Delaney of Queens, New York. How these individuals and a few other allies ganged up on President Kennedy in June 1961 to help kill an aid-to-education bill which did not include assistance to parochial schools is related in admirable detail in the Drew Pearson–Jack Anderson book *The Case Against Congress*. Briefly, President Kennedy, seeking to carry out his campaign pledge that he would observe the constitutional guarantee of separation of church and state, proposed federal aid to education and excluded the parochial schools. Cardinal Spellman put up a squawk, as did many Catholic legislators, one of whom was Speaker McCormack, whom Mr. Kennedy was wont to call "the Bishop of Boston." Cardinal Spellman forthwith convinced White House advisers that they should include aid to Catholic schools that taught math, science and languages "on the grounds that these subjects were an aid to national defense" and would not violate the principle of church–state separation. Mr. Kennedy, at first opposed to this, finally agreed to accept it. When the information got out, Protestant churchmen were up in arms, accusing the President of going back on his word. Speaker McCormack, working in close harmony with Cardinal Spellman, saw to it that the education bill got mired down in the House Rules Committee. As Congressman Carl Elliott of Alabama put it, "Cardinal Spellman killed the bill as surely as if he had come here and voted against it."

Pearson and Anderson closed their account with the following paragraph:

> Thus ended all attempts to pass a federal aid-to-education bill until after the death of President Kennedy. He

had made a valiant attempt, but then compromised beyond the point that Protestant churchmen and millions of Protestants had believed he would when they voted for him in 1960. Even so, he was unable to push an aid-to-education bill past Cardinal Spellman and the key bloc of Catholic Congressmen who wielded such substantial power . . .*

Such proposed legislation as the aid-to-education bill brings out all the big guns, but every legislator likes to know ahead of time what the "Catholic position" will be on any given issue or bill, especially one that pertains to religion. One of the most delicate issues that Congress has to face from time to time is the problem of U. S. relations with the state of Vatican City. The United States has never sent an ambassador or minister to that state, though there have been several Presidents who sent personal representatives to the Vatican. Since Uncle Sam holds to the concept of the separation of church and state, and since the state of Vatican City is the most complete union of church and state in the world, American Presidents have of necessity avoided this hot potato. So, too, has Congress.

On the question of diplomatic relations with the Vatican, Congress had an opportunity to bring the issue to a head in 1951. President Harry S Truman, having nominated General Mark Clark to be ambassador to the Vatican State, needed Senate confirmation. But the Senate was not receptive, partially because of what President Franklin D. Roosevelt had done in 1939. Roosevelt had appointed Myron Taylor as his "personal representative" to the Pope, in that way bypassing the Senate with its constitutional prerogative to confirm all ambassadors. Even though the Senate had no chance to approve or disapprove Mr. Taylor, he still used the American Embassy in Rome as his office and received assistance from State Depart-

* Drew Pearson and Jack Anderson, The Case Against Congress (New York: Simon and Schuster, 1968), p. 363.

ment employees. The Vatican gave Mr. Taylor ambassadorial status, and the betwixt-and-between envoy stayed at his post in Rome until 1950.

In the Mark Clark incident, President Truman waited until the closing period of the session of Congress to send in his nomination. There being no time to discuss the appointment before adjournment, all hell broke loose. Despite support from Catholic bishops and a number of influential daily papers, the assault against Mr. Truman was tremendous. Even the Chief Executive's own pastor linked himself to the opposition. General Clark finally did "the graceful thing" and withdrew his name—much to the relief of Congress, which had not wanted to provide a vote of record on an "anti-Catholic" issue.

President Nixon, on the other hand, has demonstrated a bit more boldness in his relations with the Vatican. Not only did he visit Pope Paul at the Vatican on two occasions, with world television cameras recording almost every step and movement, but he appointed Henry Cabot Lodge to be his personal envoy and visit the Pope two or three times a year for the purpose of exchanging information and ideas. Mr. Lodge's initial meeting with Pope Paul in July 1970 was the first completely nonceremonial meeting with a Pope by an American Presidential aide since Mr. Taylor stepped down in 1950.

When countries such as the United States do not have formal diplomatic relations with the Vatican but maintain a friendly liaison and a mutual respect for each other, the Pope does not appoint an ambassador (nuncio) to represent him, but an Apostolic Delegate, whose duty it is to watch over the condition of the Church in the territory assigned to him. Like an ambassador, the Apostolic Delegate keeps the Pontiff informed about the area. Although the Apostolic Delegate is not a diplomatic envoy in the technical sense of the word, the United States extends diplomatic courtesies to him, as do fifteen other countries.

The post of Apostolic Delegate to the United States was established by Pope Leo XII in 1893. At the very outset this Apostolic Delegate was granted the power of final decision-making in matters involving diocesan problems. To understand this delegation of power by the Pope to another man, one must understand that for a long time the Catholic clergy in the United States lived through a state of confusion, largely because there was an absence of a central administrative authority on American soil. This confusion was heightened by the innumerable immigrant divisions of the Church, using different languages and often pursuing nationalistic interests that competed with one another. Even today there remains a degree of antipathy between Irish-American Catholics (who dominate the American clergy, especially at the top) and three other large ethnic groups—Italian-American, Polish-American and German-American Catholics. This rivalry is understandable, since the internal political power of the American Catholic Church is to all intents and purposes vested in the hands of Americans of Irish background. Witness the fact that the heavy majority of the clergy, including the cardinals and the archbishops, is of Irish descent. This "Irishization" of the American Church has for nearly a century been a thorn in the side of the Vatican.

Thus it is no wonder that the Apostolic Delegate who occupies the spacious building at 1312 Massachusetts Avenue, the general headquarters of the Catholic Church in America, is and has always been an Italian. In this way the Pope makes sure that the "Irish heresy" of American Catholicism remains under the control of a man whose first allegiance is to Rome.

The current Apostolic Delegate to the U. S. is Archbishop Luigi Raimondi. Archbishop Raimondi, who was born in October 1912 at Lussito, Italy, was secretary of the apostolic nunciature in Guatemala from 1938 to 1942, secretary and auditor of the apostolic delegation in the U. S. from 1942 to

1949 and auditor of the apostolic internunciature in India from 1949 to 1953, and he was appointed papal Nuncio to Haiti in 1953. In 1956 he became the Apostolic Delegate to Mexico, where he remained until 1967, at which time he went to Washington to take up his present duties.

Like his predecessors, Archbishop Raimondi prefers to keep out of the journalistic spotlight. His name therefore, rarely gets into the papers. That is not always an easy trick for a man at his level of importance. In the summer of 1970 he was drawn into the news columns when 350 delegates to the first national convention of black lay Catholics marched in angry unison to his residence and demanded that four regional black dioceses be established, with a black bishop elected by black Catholics. Excoriating the Apostolic Delegate because there was "little resemblance between the Catholic religion and the Gospel of Jesus Christ," the militant group wanted Archbishop Raimondi to know that although American Negro Catholics are a distinct minority (numbering about 800,000 out of a total U. S. Catholic population of about 47.8 million), the Church had let them down.* The Archbishop said that the requests would be brought to the attention of His Holiness in Rome.

Such matters of a social nature are the concern of an Apos-

* Another Negro group in the nation's capital recently confronted Patrick Cardinal O'Boyle, Archbishop of Washington. The Black United Front wanted Cardinal O'Boyle to make a full disclosure of archdiocesan and parochial finances, including real-estate holdings, investments and all income and disbursements. The group pointed out that while 50,000 Washington families live in poverty and slum housing, the archdiocese proceeds with another $4 million worth of church construction. Challenging the Cardinal to get on with the business of providing money to build up parts of Washington, the Black United Front asked the archdiocese to deed over to it six lots on Seventh Street, N.W., a mansion on the northeast corner of Sixteenth Street, a huge apartment building at Western Avenue and Thirty-seventh Street N.W., and eleven commercial lots on the north side of F Street. They also demanded that the Catholic Bishops of America raise $4 million for a Black Development Bank in the District of Columbia.

tolic Delegate, but his influence is equally felt in economic affairs, especially if he is an expert in these matters. Such a man was Egidio Cardinal Vagnozzi. Having served as the Apostolic Delegate to the U. S. for nine years, Cardinal Vagnozzi is today the Vatican's "finance minister" in Rome and oversees the extensive business operations of the Vatican. It was Pope John XXIII who appointed him as the Apostolic Delegate to the U. S. to replace Amleto Cardinal Cicognani when the latter when back to Rome to take up his duties as Vatican Secretary of State. Although Cardinal Vagnozzi was formally trained in philosophy and theology, he became a sharp observer of the American economy and a keen admirer of the "American way of doing business." He is the only cardinal in history to have visited all of the fifty states, and it is believed that no other single person inside the Vatican has his incisive knowledge of American business practices and the U. S. economy today.

It was Cardinal Vagnozzi who gave "a negative report" to the Vatican on President John F. Kennedy. Involved in the report was a little-publicized incident that took place in November 1961 when Cardinal Cicognani, the former Apostolic Delegate who had become Vatican Secretary of State, made an attempt to see the President on the occasion of a return visit to the United States. On applying for an appointment for a courtesy call to the Chief Executive, the Cardinal was informed that Mr. Kennedy was occupied with pressing matters. A second attempt by His Eminence was also frustrated by the White House, which said that the United States government did not officially recognize the Vatican government and that a visit by its Cardinal Secretary of State would embarrass the President.

Deciding to pull some strings, the then Bishop Vagnozzi persuaded Cardinal Cicognani to stay in Washington an extra day and then got a prominent figure in the Kennedy Administration, who was a convert to Catholicism, to try to set up a meeting. The White House finally yielded and made an appointment for the Holy See's Secretary of State, on condition that the visit be classified as a personal one. Accompanied by Apostolic Delegate Vagnozzi, Cardinal Cicognani arrived at the back door of the White House (as per instructions) and was escorted to the front door, where the President greeted him formally. During the approximately twenty minutes that Mr. Kennedy stayed with the Vatican's representatives, news photographers were denied an opportunity to take pictures.

During his long residence in Washington as Apostolic Delegate, Cardinal Cicognani had been received by several Presidents of Protestant affiliation. The Catholic officer, therefore, had not expected the White House to give him a cold shoulder. But things got worse. Eight days later, when Protestant evangelist Billy Graham paid a courtesy call on President Kennedy, the carpet was literally laid out for him, in spite of the fact that Mr. Graham had gone to bat for Richard Nixon during the 1960 Presidential campaign. Bishop Vagnozzi became even more disenchanted with J.F.K., a practicing Roman Catholic, when Mr. Kennedy refused to grant federal aid to parochial schools. Inside the Vatican the name of John F. Kennedy had become mud. "Protestant Presidents like Hoover, Roosevelt, Truman and Eisenhower," the Apostolic Delegate is known to have said at the time, "were more charitable toward us than the present occupant of the White House."

9

WHERE THERE'S A WILL . . .

A will is a solemn matter . . . with men whose life is given up to business.—MILLARD FILLMORE

WHEN SARITA KENEDY EAST died of cancer in February 1961 at the age of seventy-one in New York City, she left behind a fortune worth close to $300 million. Her death set off a series of legal tangles between two rival groups of Roman Catholics, a bitter war of words and wits that echoed all the way to the Vatican. The trouble emerged as a result of three wills made by Mrs. East, an eccentric widow and a Roman Catholic with strong charitable motivations. Therein lie many of the complications that have stirred up a nest of fees.

The story of Mrs. East began with her grandfather, Captain Miflin Kenedy, who with a fellow boatman acquired vast holdings of land in southern Texas at the end of the Civil War. After the two men split up, Captain Kenedy's 400,000 acres became known as the Kenedy Ranch, which he willed to his son John. John had two children—a son, John Junior, and a daughter, Sarita, who in 1910 married Arthur Lee East. In 1931 when John Senior died, he left 200,000 acres to each of his two children. Neither Sarita's marriage nor her brother's produced an heir. In 1944, after her husband died, Mrs. East wrote her first will, leaving her 200,000 acres, which she had named the La Parra Ranch, to her brother. But in 1948 he died, and in December of that year Mrs. East decided to write a new will. This second testament left the bulk of her property to her nearest kin, her first cousins Edgar Turcotte and Mrs. Stella Turcotte Lytton, with whom she had grown up and with whom she enjoyed a close relationship.

During the 1950s there were new developments at the La Parra Ranch. The Humble Oil Company, which had leased La Parra's 200,000 acres, discovered a large oil and gas deposit on Mrs. East's property. Concerned that federal death taxes would take too big a chunk from her estate, Mrs. East set about creating a charitable foundation, which would allow the ranch to be kept in operation after her death. As a memorial to her late parents, she established the foundation as a nonprofit Texas corporation in January 1960. A few weeks later, in February, she wrote her third and last will, leaving the bulk of her estate to the foundation. Mrs. East died a year later.

Before her death, however, Mrs. East met a Trappist monk called Brother Leo, of the St. Joseph Abbey in Spencer, Massachusetts. Brother Leo, born Roderick Norton Gregory in Berkeley, California, in 1917, joined the Trappist order while in his junior year at Loyola University in Los Angeles. Though he began his monastic life as a shoemaker, he soon displayed another talent that was to be of greater use to the order—that of a fund raiser. The work of soliciting financial help from wealthy Catholics took Brother Leo to all parts of the United States and to several foreign countries. And ultimately he met Sarita Kenedy East.

At the time, he was raising money for two Trappist monasteries that were being set up in Argentina and Chile. Developing an extreme fondness for Brother Leo, Mrs. East arranged for his lodging on her ranch while she marshaled the legal tools for disposing of her estate. In time she gave the personable monk power of attorney. And in June 1960, to the surprise of everyone, Mrs. East removed three members from the board of directors of her foundation, the Roman Catholic Bishop of Corpus Christi, Texas, one of her cousins and her lawyer, and substituted three other persons—Brother Leo, a millionaire Catholic president of a large shipping line, and the founder of a prayer-crusading society known as the Family Rosary, Inc. Eight months later, with Brother Leo at her bedside, Mrs. East succumbed to cancer. With her death began the legal squabble.

Her two cousins, heirs under her second will, sought to void the last will and to have the 1948 will probated instead. About a hundred of Mrs. East's distant relatives, who lived in various parts of the United States and Mexico, bid for the will's residuary clause to be nullified and the bulk of the estate distributed among them instead of to the foundation. The Corpus Christi Diocese sought to have the first codicil to the 1960 will probated instead of the third codicil (which took away the bishop's membership in the foundation's board of directors, granted in the first codicil). The diocese also sued for a voice in how the proceeds should be dispersed. Eventually the Vatican felt impelled to intervene, and early in 1962 it ordered Brother Leo to withdraw all actions in the case in line with his obligations, while Archbishop John J. Krol of Philadelphia, who had been appointed apostolic visitor by Pope John XXIII, attempted to settle the matter on amicable terms.

However, Brother Leo defied the Vatican. Refusing to remain silent, he took the position that his conscience rebelled against settlement because he felt in his heart that it was Mrs. East's intention to have him continue to play a dominant role in overseeing her estate. Because he continued to disobey Church orders, the Trappists eventually defrocked him.

Until the matter is finally settled, the courts have frozen the estate and its mounting income, which averages around $100,-000 a month and has brought in nearly $3 million extra during the long-drawn-out litigations.

Although the case of Mrs. East made continuous headlines—and is likely to make a few more before the issue is settled—most of the wills involving the Catholic Church get little or no publicity. A case in point is the $2.4-million bequest left to the late William Cardinal O'Connell of the Boston Archdiocese in 1923 by A. Paul Keith, a theater magnate. The Cardinal was a trustee of the estate for eighteen years, and it was only after he died in 1944, when an accounting was filed for the first time, that the bequest was given any space in the Boston papers. The accounting showed that the original bequest had increased through investments to approximately $3.5 million. Mr. Keith, son of the founder of a chain of theaters bearing his name, left the bequest to the Cardinal with the stipulation that the proceeds be "spent for the benefit of such charitable purposes as he may deem best." Disbursements listed in the statement were construction, $1.3 million; educational contributions, $868,285; charitable contributions, $558,-572; religious contributions, $320,810; and miscellaneous contributions, $46,669. An important item in the disbursements was the construction of the archbishop's residence, on which $412,343 was spent.

As might be surmised from the foregoing instances, the Catholic Church will actively pursue a situation where it can become the beneficiary of a will. Members of the clergy in many dioceses throughout the country exhort their parishioners not to forget the Church in making out their testaments. Some priests even send letters to lawyers asking them to remind clients that a good Catholic is expected to bequeath his Church at least 10 percent of the legacy. One diocese went to the trouble and expense of printing up a fifty-two-page booklet to provide guidance along these lines. The Diocese of

Dallas–Fort Worth (which just recently split into two separate entities) published the handbook to help Roman Catholics who would want information on the preparation and management of wills, trusts, annuities, deeds, gifts, memorials and taxes on gifts to the Church. On the first page the text states that the book was published "in the hope that many will be inspired by what is written here to return to Christ some portion of the material means they have enjoyed." The chapter devoted to wills, called "A Good Catholic Makes a Good Will," urges the reader in low key to do the will of God with what material things he cannot take with him to the grave. It goes on to say:

> He has first the natural obligation to provide for members of his own family. He has also at death the supernatural obligation, as he has had in life, to leave something for the work of God's Church after he has gone to his reward. It is far easier to appear before the judgment seat of God if you are secure in the knowledge that your love of neighbor, which is love of God, did not end at the grave. . . . The responsibility of performing the works of mercy does not end at the funeral Mass. It should be anticipated for all time. Our personal works of mercy should go on after death. There is no better monument.

How much money is left to the Catholic Church in the United States each year cannot be ascertained with accuracy. The estimates range between $500 million and $1 billion, all of which is tax-free, but this naturally must fluctuate from year to year. Although most of the bequests are rather modest, occasionally the newspapers report cases in which substantial sums are left. For instance, several years ago Ruth T. Wallace of Saratoga Springs, New York, left $2.5 million to Pope Paul and another $2.5 million to the Redemptorist Fathers of New

York. When she died at the age of 62, unmarried, Miss Wallace's estate consisted of investments, cash and large parcels of land.

Sometimes the money tables are turned, however. There was in Avon, Ohio, the case of a priest, the Reverend John C. Schaefer, who left the bulk of his $262,000 estate to his housekeeper of more than twenty years. A token sum of less than $1,000 was directed to several parishes, but most of the money went to Miss Ann Masimer. Father Schaefer left her $111,403 in cash, a home valued at $21,900, and securities and stocks that were worth $102,485.

Although it does what it can to keep a public spotlight away from its money operations, the Catholic Church has demonstrated that it is never reluctant to go into a courtroom and engage in a tug-of-war, no matter how much attention the case may attract in the newspapers. Battles over wills constitute good examples of how tenacious the Catholic Church can be in the courts. With the exception of these will fights, Catholic court battles at the federal or state level have nearly always involved tax-exemption litigations.

Indeed, government is a prime source of income for the Catholic Church. And whenever there is a challenge to the Church's receiving government money or benefiting from a tax ruling, the Catholic authorities are quick to take up the cudgels—with a good chance of emerging the victors. However strong some of the litigations against the Church may have been, court decisions nearly always have been based on precedents, which generally favor the Church. Yet, you can't win 'em all. . . .

There is, for example, the case involving the Brothers of Christian Instruction in York County, Maine, in which the county commissioner rejected the Church's appeal for tax exemption. The county had imposed taxes on the Brothers' real-estate and personal property because the Catholic order had been deriving income from selling bread, chickens, eggs and milk. In still another case, the Daughters of St. Paul attempted to get an exemption from the ad-valorem tax on a bookstore that also sold gifts. A court in San Antonio, Texas, ruling against them, held that a nonprofit corporation "which owned a building used exclusively by the corporation for sale of books and for nuns' living quarters was not, under the facts, an 'institution of purely public charity' so as to be exempt from city and school district taxes."

A commercially run cafeteria inside the Shrine of the Immaculate Conception in Washington, D.C., came into prominence when the Shrine was assessed personal-property taxes on equipment in the cafeteria. In 1962 the Catholic Church took the case to court and won an exemption of $4,079, which had already been paid. A district-court judge ordered the money refunded. Citing a law exempting from personal-property taxes all benevolent organizations "not conducted for private gain," the judge held that although the cafeteria business had reported annual profits, the Shrine itself was not being operated for private gain.

In another suit, A. J. Simler of North Little Rock, Arkansas, sought to break the will of his sister, Mrs. Birdine Fletcher of Oklahoma City, who had bequeathed "one dollar, this amount and no more" to her brother and the bulk of her estate to the Catholic Church when she died in 1952. Mrs. Fletcher left 160 acres of her Caddo County farm, which had twelve producing oil wells valued at $210,000, to the Sisters of St. Francis of Maryville, Missouri. She also left $50,000 to St. Anthony Hospital (where she died), $10,000 to the St. Joseph Orphanage, and $5,000 to St. Patrick's Mission. Mr. Simler fought the case through various courts. First he contested the will, alleging that Mrs. Fletcher was an incompetent when she died and was under "undue influence" when she made out her will a week before her death. After the courts upheld the will,

Mr. Simler challenged the legality of a foreign corporation's (the Catholic order) taking title to property not within an incorporated city or town. The U.S. Court of Appeals ruled in favor of Mr. Simler on the ground that both the Oklahoma Constitution and a state law forbid the holding of land outside cities and towns by organizations for purposes other than those for which they were chartered. Specifically, the ruling stated that the Sisters of St. Francis could not legally maintain land for oil and gas production since they, as a corporation, had not been created to deal in a business of this kind. The Caddo farm land had produced income in excess of $475,000, noted the court, which valued the farm at $879,926 at the time of the decision.

When the city of Rochester, Minnesota, made an effort to tax the Madonna Towers Retirement Home, run by the Oblate Fathers, the Roman Catholic order brought the case to court, in February 1968. The Oblate Fathers won their suit on the contention that the twelve-story apartment building, with its nine adjacent town houses, an infirmary, a dining hall, a chapel, a recreation center and a solarium, was a "purely public charity" and hence entitled to exemption from taxes. The case was appealed to the Minnesota Supreme Court on the grounds that heavy entrance fees were required and that substantial rental charges were made. In March 1969 that court reversed the lower court, stating that Madonna Towers was not a purely public charity.

The Missionary Sisters Servants of the Holy Spirit and the Society for the Divine Word, two Roman Catholic organizations in Chicago, jointly own 186 acres of land, a few miles outside the city, that became a public issue. In the summer of 1964 Lake Land Fill, Inc., contracted with them to use the land for a "sanitary-fill" operation on the owners' assurance that the zoning would be changed from its then single-family category to an industrial category with a special use as a dump. Because the nearby communities had previously had unpleasant experiences with garbage-dumping operations, the proposal aroused violent protests, despite the fact that modern facilities to alleviate nuisances were promised. So great was the public uproar that the zoning-board hearing on the matter took three days. The crux of the controversy was that although the communities were running out of places to dump their refuse, nobody wanted a dump near his particular community. It was complicated by another factor—land available for landfill is extremely valuable because the topsoil can be sold and, in effect, the "hole" can then be sold for dumping.

In May 1965 the zoning board finally rejected the change of category in a detailed nine-page report. The key argument cited was that sanitary landfills attract sea gulls in winter and that these birds would be a constant threat to flying operations at the nearby airport. Behind the scenes the two Catholic orders which owned the disputed land parcel exercised some political pressures and got the County Board to agree to restudy the zoning board's decision. New evidence was submitted that disputed the sea gull–menace argument. Federal authorites also got interested in the case and opted for a new zoning classification. In September 1965 the zoning appeal board reviewed the case and once again refused to recommend a zoning change. A month later the County Board voted to uphold the zoning board's recommendations. The owners of the land parcel then took the case to court.

The Cook County Circuit Court in 1967 overturned the county zoning board's ruling, so the county and two villages (Northbrook and Glenview) appealed to the State Appellate Court, which in March 1969 upheld the decision by ruling that the county zoning board's refusal to allow a landfill on the disputed site was unconstitutional. Today there is no longer an issue as to whether the site is a garbage dump or a sanitary landfill, for some eighty-five garbage trucks arrive each day between 9 A.M. and 3 P.M. to dispose of their refuse. The site, which is shielded by an eight-foot wooden fence, will take another ten years to fill. At the end of that time the level of the ground will have been raised eight feet, and the land can be reclaimed for farming.

The financial saga of a Milwaukee-based order of nuns is another chapter in Catholic business history that warrants close inspection. In this case, the Society of the Divine Saviour, a religious order incorporated in Wisconsin, engaged in a get-rich-quick scheme. Convinced that it could double or perhaps triple its existing capital, the Society entrusted its hopes to a Washington lawyer, Victor J. Orsinger, a prominent Catholic layman. At his advice, it acquired a plush real-estate development near Washington called Parkwood, Inc. The order invested a little over $4 million in this project, but the company never became a growing concern, and it died. Three million dollars of the money lost had come from the nuns' sale of unregistered bonds that had been donated to a fund-raising drive of theirs to build a seminary in Rome and to support missionary work in Africa—projects which never got under way.

Both Mr. Orsinger and the Society apparently were willing to throw good money after bad in an attempt to recoup their losses. Mr. Orsinger became mixed up with the Janaf Shopping Center, a multimillion-dollar operation in Norfolk, Virginia, which for nearly a decade has been the subject of a legal wrangle. The Janaf affair eventually brought on a complaint filed by the Securities and Exchange Commission in a federal district court in 1966, charging that Mr. Orsinger and his associates had been and were then "employing devices, schemes and artifices to defraud and engaging in transactions, practices and a course of business which would and did operate as a fraud upon certain persons."

The man who conceived the Janaf Shopping Center ("Janaf" stands for Joint Army–Navy–Air Force) was retired Lieutenant Commander James K. Beazley, who in 1954 found 914 servicemen willing to invest some of their money in a real-estate deal. Although Commander Beazley's idea eventually became a "fabulous economic success" (currently valued at approximately $11 million), he and his 914 military partners have gained nothing from it and have apparently lost their original investment of $600,000. Commander Beazley, in a $15-million suit, has charged the Milwaukee nuns with fraud. Named also in the Beazley affidavit is Mr. Orsinger—who meanwhile, in the fall of 1969, was found guilty on nine counts in a criminal indictment charging him with defrauding the Sisters of the Divine Saviour of $1.5 million, a decision which has since been appealed.

According to Commander Beazley's bill of complaint, Mr. Orsinger, as financial adviser to the Society, arranged two short-term loans and one long-term loan from the Society to Janaf. The two short-term loans were for $500,000 and $350,-000, while the other loan was in the amount of $350,000. Commander Beazley said that Mr. Orsinger had to borrow back $125,000 temporarily for the Society, a sum that was supposed to have been returned in thirty days. But, according to the suit, Mr. Orsinger failed to repay the money at the end of the month and asserted that the $125,000 was merely a partial repayment of the loan. Commander Beazley maintains that the withdrawal of this $125,000 caused Janaf to lose two $650,000 permanent-loan commitments from an insurance company and a bank, bringing on delay in the construction of a Janaf motel, a rise in building costs and a loss of income.

Commander Beazley's suit points out that because Mr. Orsinger was "unable to return the $125,000," the latter procured from the Society a commitment in writing to lend Janaf $900,000. The retired naval officer maintains that Mr. Orsinger "concealed" the fact that a $900,000 loan "would exhaust practically all of the funds in the Society's annuity fund" and also "concealed that the Society was at that time indebted to the Chemical Bank in the amount of $600,000."

"Both Mr. Orsinger and the Society concealed from Janaf," adds Commander Beazley in his affidavit, "that ten shopping center notes on or about June 1957 had been pledged and delivered to the Chemical Bank as partial collateral for loans to the Society, that the Society was without funds to pay these debts to the said bank from their own resources and that said notes were no longer held by defendants . . ."

A number of financial transactions followed, as well as a suit by Mr. Orsinger against Janaf and Commander Beazley over ownership of shares of capital stock (representing 97 percent ownership). A court judgment in Washington—later upheld in the U. S. Court of Appeals and denied review by the U. S. Supreme Court—ruled in favor of Mr. Orsinger. Commander Beazley insists, however, that this judgment was "obtained by fraud upon the court" because Mr. Orsinger was "not holder of the notes sued upon." According to the Orsinger side of the case, Commander Beazley's suit has no merit because the issues were already resolved in the Washington court. But Commander Beazley contends that "at no time has there ever been a hearing on the merits of Janaf's claims in any court, due to the conspiracy of Mr. Orsinger and the condonance of the Society."

10

WALKING THE PAROCHIAID TIGHTROPE

Leave the matter of religion to the family altar, the church, and the private school, supported entirely by private contributions. Keep the church and the state forever separate.
—ULYSSES S. GRANT

JULY 1949 was a hot month even for New York, and the temperature was not lowered by Francis Cardinal Spellman's response to Mrs. Eleanor Roosevelt in her nationally syndicated column, "My Day," regarding the separation of church and state. She had written:

> The controversy brought about by the request made by Francis Cardinal Spellman that Catholic schools should share in federal aid funds forces upon the citizens of the country the kind of decision that is going to be very difficult to make. Those of us who believe in the right of any human being to belong to whatever church he sees fit, and to worship God in his own way, cannot be accused of prejudice when we do not want to see public education connected with religious control of the schools, which are paid for by taxpayers' money. . . .

Many years ago it was decided that the public schools of our country should be entirely separated from any kind of denominational control, and these are the only schools that are free, tax-supported schools. The greatest number of our children attend these schools. . . . The separation of church and state is extremely important to any of us who hold to the original traditions of our nation. To change these traditions by changing our traditional attitude toward public education would be harmful, I think, to our whole attitude of tolerance in the religious area.

Cardinal Spellman responded quickly, charging Mrs. Roosevelt with "spinning and spreading a web of prejudice." In a letter to her which was made public, the prominent clergyman wrote: "For whatever you may say in the future, your record of anti-Catholicism stands for all to see—a record which you yourself wrote on the pages of history which cannot be recalled—documents of discrimination unworthy of an American mother."

It should be noted that Cardinal Spellman later apologized to Mrs. Roosevelt and added to these views by issuing a long statement to the New York newspapers in which he said:

It is important that everyone should understand clearly what we are asking for under constitutional law, and, for what we are not asking. We are not asking for general public support of religious schools. In the State of New York, as in practically every other state, the State Constitution prohibits the use of public funds for support of sectarian schools. The Supreme Court of the United States has interpreted the Federal Constitution in the same sense. Under the Constitution we do not ask nor can we expect public funds to pay for the construction or repair of parochial school buildings or for the support of teachers, or for other maintenance costs. There are, however, other incidental expenses involved in education. . . . These are called "auxiliary services." The federal-aid controversy revolves around these incidental benefits to school children, and around them alone.

The Mrs. Roosevelt–Cardinal Spellman incident in 1949 presaged the current legislative battles over the issue of state aid to parochial schools. During Lyndon B. Johnson's administration, Congress passed and the President signed the Federal Elementary and Secondary Education Act, which siphoned an annual $286 million into sectarian schools throughout the country. Of this, $258 million a year is tabbed for schools belonging to Catholic organizations. With such sums of federal money going into parochial schools, outcries are being raised at the state and municipal level over the issue. As these words are being written, the future of nonpublic schools hangs in the balance in a majority of the states, for Catholic schools and Catholic school systems in every state and in just about every city and town are hurting for money. Campaigns to get state tax funds for the support of Catholic schools have moved into high gear all across the country. Bishop after bishop, monsignor after monsignor, pastor after pastor are bemoaning the financial situations in which diocesan schools find themselves. Catholic newspapers in every one of the fifty states show intense concern for the future of parochial-school education. And the cause of the crisis is always the same—loss of religious personnel to staff the schools, resulting in the employment of lay teachers. If teacher salary costs continue to rise, it is apparent that most of the Catholic schools in America will eventually shut down unless state aid is forthcoming.

State legislators are swamped with figures to show how taxes would increase if parochial schools closed down and dumped all their pupils into the public-school systems. Yet a look at some statistics shows that this would not necessarily follow. Catholic schools in the United States, according to figures made available for the fall 1969 semester, enrolled about 5 million pupils, or about 9 percent of the nation's schoolchildren, who number some 51.5 million. Were only half of the Catholic schools to close, the increase in enrollment in the public schools would be less than 5 percent. Even if all the Catholic schools were to close in the next decade, it would not put an undue burden on the existing public schools. This is so partly because in the next ten years there will be a tremendous dip in the number of schoolchildren, due to America's declining birth rate during the 1960s. In July 1969, as a result of the lowering birth rate, there were 2.3 million fewer children under the age of five than there were in the same month in 1960.

These are the views expressed in some quarters which maintain that because of that decline of more than two million in the number of children, at least a million youngsters from the parochial schools could be absorbed without the hiring of additional teaching personnel or the addition of more classrooms. Thus the question of a higher tax burden on the public to support education appears to be more a matter of propaganda than one of fact. Only in such cities as Boston, Chicago, New York and Philadelphia, where there are large numbers of Catholic schools, might undue hardship be imposed on the cities' public-school systems.

But still, despite a national public relations campaign, opinion in the United States is apparently running against the use of state monies for parochial schools. For instance, a Gallup Poll survey in 1966 (on the question "People who send their children to religious schools pay taxes for the support of the public schools, as well as paying for the support of the religious schools. Do you think public taxes should be used to support the religious schools also, or not?") indicated that a majority of Americans disapproved of using public funds for parochial schools. A comparison of the tabulations of this survey with those of a similar Gallup survey done in 1952 showed that the percentage of those opposed to such aid had risen. In 1952, 40 percent of those polled voted Yes on the use of state funds for religious schools, and 49 percent voted No. In 1966, 38 percent voted Yes, 50 percent No. The latest available poll, also conducted by Gallup, showed that 59 percent of those queried opposed public subsidy for students in nonpublic education and only 38 percent favored it.

Equally significant is the evidence that most Roman Catholics do not want to be taxed for their Church's schools. That the Catholics of New York State do not want state aid for their schools is borne out by the results of a 1967 referendum on a proposed new state constitution whose most hotly contested provision was one allowing public funds to go to parochial schools. A heavy effort was made to get out the Catholic vote in favor of the proposed constitution. Mass meetings were held in each of New York's fifty-seven senatorial districts. Pulling out all the stops, Cardinal Spellman staged a huge rally in Madison Square Garden at which he exhorted followers to vote for the new constitution, and where the Cardinal declared that the possibility that the legislation might not go through presented "the gravest crisis in the history of the Catholic Church in America." Throughout the state the Catholic dioceses formed "Fairness to Children" committees which distributed literature, got people to write letters and urged Catholic voters to register for the November election. Some $3 million was spent for newspaper and television advertising on behalf of the new constitution. Additional money was spent to make a color propaganda film focusing on the issue of public aid to parochial schools, and this movie was shown in every Catholic church in the state. Two days before the referendum, a letter from Cardinal Spellman urging support for the new charter was read at all Masses in every church in the New York Archdiocese.

This mammoth effort did not work, however. By a vote of nearly three to one, the proposed constitution was defeated. It failed to carry a single borough of New York City; in fact, it failed in every one of the state's sixty-two counties. Observers at the time commented that in a state that is 41 percent Roman Catholic the two-to-one No vote in New York City and the four-to-one No vote throughout the rest of the state showed clearly that the people were solidly against state aid to parochial schools.

An organization of Catholics that is unequivocally opposed to state aid to parochial schools is the National Association of Laymen. This group bases its opposition on three points: the diverse viewpoints on this issue within the Catholic community, the inadequate financial data reported by Church officers, and the increasing sentiment in favor of phasing out parochial schools. The N.A.L. claims that though it does not speak for all the laity in the country, it does represent a significant and growing number of mainstream Catholics who oppose government aid to church schools. It has stated:

Contrary to the general impression, Catholics are not united on the issue of state aid to parochial schools. Actually there is a marked cleavage on this matter. The extent of this cleavage is not apparent because traditional structures in parishes and dioceses do not generally allow open dialogue on issues where the bishops have taken a strong stand. However, where structures for free discussion do exist, as in Detroit, it soon becomes obvious that many Catholics are strongly opposed to state aid to parochial schools. The Detroit Association of Laymen, an affiliate of N.A.L., publicly opposed Parochiaid . . . and was instrumental in securing its narrow defeat in the state

185

legislature. As more and more lay associations throughout the country take a stand on this issue, it will become clear that the cleavage is far greater than is generally supposed.

Holding to the view that legislators and voters should be aware that financial data offered by Church officers in support of state aid to parochial schools may not reflect the complete financial situation, and annoyed that Catholic laity have been rebuffed in their attempts to secure meaningful fiscal data, the N.A.L. in June 1969 adopted some resolutions on financial accountability. These read as follows:

> Whereas vast sums of money are contributed by lay Catholics to the support of parishes, dioceses, various Catholic institutions and the Vatican; and whereas the control of these funds is solely and exclusively in the hands of clergy who are not required to make an accounting to the lay persons who contribute the funds . . . and whereas Catholics cannot make intelligent decisions about whether to support these institutions unless they know the scope of present assets and needs of the institutions, now therefore be it resolved that (1) the N.A.L. reaffirm its position of a year ago calling for full and open financial disclosure, subject to public audit, by all church institutions on all levels; (2) N.A.L. continue a vigorous campaign to compel financial disclosure in all dioceses of the U. S.; (3) N.A.L. call for formation of a broad-based national committee of clergy and lay people to assist bishops of the U. S. in establishing and implementing procedures for full disclosure and to conduct public hearings exploring the wishes of all segments of the U. S. church.

Since the N.A.L. holds to the view that the parochial system has outlived its usefulness, the members are united in their belief that all Catholic elementary and secondary schools should undergo a gradual phasing-out process and that as buildings, personnel and finances are made available, they should be utilized where feasible to create parish community centers that could be used for informal religious education programs, both for children and for young adults.

Perhaps the most definitive statement against state aid to the parochial schools was made by Gaston D. Cogdell, America's leading scholar on the subject, in his book *What Price Parochiaid?* * Basing his argument on the initial stipulation of the first article of the Bill of Rights, Mr. Cogdell declares:

> No government has the right to force any man to support the activities of any church—not even his own, much less someone else's. No church has the right to accept coerced support for any of its activities, even from its own members. How much less does it have the right to impose the cost of its schools or other institutions upon those who do not subscribe to, or who are opposed to, its doctrines and structure of ecclesiastical authority?

Meanwhile, as the controversy goes on, Catholic schools over the country are undergoing an "erosion" which, year by year, is forcing additional thousands of children into the public schools. Facing a dollar crunch, America's Catholic schools are victims of sharply rising costs and a diminishing supply of teachers from religious orders. Having previously relied mainly on nuns to do the teaching—at a cost of about $1,200 a year per nun—the Catholic schools have had to go out into the marketplace and compete with the public schools for lay teachers, above all for those specializing in the sciences, who are hard to come by. The recent decline in the number of American Catholics entering religious vocations and the in-

* Published by Americans United, Washington, D.C., 1970. (The word "Parochiaid" is a neologism for the use of public funds for parochial schools.)

creasing number of priests and members of religious orders resigning because they do not want to live under medieval rules of supervision have had a drastic effect on the teaching ranks of the Catholic school systems. Today Catholic schools employ over 90,000 lay teachers; contrast this with the approximately 35,000 lay teachers they employed ten years ago and consider the corresponding increase in salaries, and one begins to envision what a harrowing prospect is in store for Catholic schools in the forthcoming decade.

Small wonder, then, that Catholic leaders concerned about the survival of the parochial schools in the face of mounting costs see state subsidy as the only answer. But in seeking it, they sometimes defeat themselves. In Michigan several years ago a bill to provide $21 million in tuition grants to "parents of non–public-school children" was introduced in the state legislature, and Catholic leaders and their allies went about drumming support for it. The result, paradoxically, was a setback for the bill's supporters, not for lack of public support but because of too much public enthusiasm. It was a case of political overkill provoking resentment. Catholic lobbyists and their backers organized a blitz letter-writing campaign. In one week alone, more than 200,000 letters poured into the State Capitol at Lansing. It was the biggest backing for any issue in recent Michigan history. Yet among the legislators who had not previously made up their minds the reaction was a negative one.

"It was awful," one state representative from Detroit recalled. "The whole legislative process broke down, as everybody on my staff and everyone of my colleagues' staff could do nothing else but open the mail."

Expressing disappointment at the result—the bill was never reported out of committee—one Michigan priest perhaps summed up best the dilemma of his Church. "The time has come," he lamented, "for us to take a second look at what we are doing."

Indeed, he might also have been referring to the other side of the coin, such as what happened in Indiana not long ago. There some nuns employed in public schools receive an annual salary of $7,500, but these devoted women do not pay any income tax on the money because they turn their paychecks over to the Catholic order to which they belong. When complaints were lodged with the Bureau of Internal Revenue by taxpaying lay teachers in the same schools, who claimed that "the wearing of distinctive garb does not exempt a person from the duties of citizenship," the Bureau explained there was nothing anybody could do about it, because the nuns gave all their income to their Church.

One of the disgruntled teachers wrapped up the incredible situation as follows: "If *we* wanted to do the same thing for our religion, the Bureau of Internal Revenue would not allow us to deduct more than 30 percent. What the Bureau hath joined together, let not taxpayers put asunder!"

11

THE NICE MAN COMETH

It's not John Kennedy's spiritual father [the Pope] that worries me. It's his natural father [Joe].—Harry S Truman

ONE DAY at the height of World War II, the late Joseph P. Kennedy was playing a round of golf on his private course near the Kennedy winter home at Palm Beach, Florida, when a house servant caught up with him on one of the tees to report that Cardinal Spellman was on the phone from New York. It seems the Cardinal had a problem and wanted Joe's help.

Actually, Cardinal Spellman had two problems which he thought could be cleared up by a single solution. It appeared that the New York Archdiocese would not be able to realize one of its pet projects, a new printing of the works of Saint Thomas Aquinas, because paper supplies were hard to come by. Random House, the New York publishing company, had told the Cardinal it could not take on the worthy assignment because it was unable to find enough paper. And at the time Random House had another problem of its own. The executives of the company needed new offices but were unable to find a suitable location. This provided still another reason why

Random House could not undertake a big publishing commitment at that time.

Cardinal Spellman offered to help the publishing company find new space. Hence the long-distance phone call to Mr. Kennedy in Florida. As chance would have it, Joe Kennedy had just purchased from a Wall Street colleague a block of six houses on Madison Avenue which had remained mostly empty. His proposed solution to Cardinal Spellman's distress call was immediate. He gave most of the property to the archdiocese and sold Random House one of the buildings at an inordinately low price. And ultimately, by diverting paper from other programs, Random House was able to print the Aquinas writings.

The strength and wealth of the Catholic Church in the United States derive no small assistance from a legion of well-to-do Catholic laymen like Joe Kennedy who often will not hesitate to expend prodigious amounts of cash, effort and influence on behalf of their Church. To penetrate the secret of Catholic wealth in the United States, one must go beyond the clergy and even beyond the Vatican itself. No one will dispute that an influential Catholic citizen with a generous wallet and an open mind can give substantial boosts to his local parish through his largesse. It is happening all the time. Who are some of these powerhouse Catholic laymen who form, in their own way, the third arm of the Roman Catholic Church in America?

Perhaps the richest Catholic family in the United States is the O'Shaughnessy family of St. Paul, Minnesota. The exact worth of Ignatius Aloysius O'Shaughnessy, who made hundreds of millions of dollars in oil, is anybody's guess. Mr. O'Shaughnessy bought his first wildcat well in 1910 while in Oklahoma and is today the owner of the Globe Oil & Refining Company, the largest privately held company of its kind in North America. Generous with his money, the centimillionaire has made notable bequests to the College of St. Thomas in Minnesota and contributed large sums to Notre Dame, Loyola and De Paul Universities, all of which have awarded him honorary degrees.

Not far behind in terms of family fortune, but certainly more well-known, is the Kennedy family of Massachusetts. Enough has been written about the Kennedy wealth to fill whole libraries. Joe Kennedy's fortune was variously estimated at between $250 million and half a billion—money which he made in stock speculation, the movies, liquor importing, real estate, oil ventures and corporate reorganization. Primarily, Mr. Kennedy was not interested in industry and production but rather in stocks and securities. He pulled out of the stock market months before the 1929 crash and made more millions by selling short. After the Second World War Mr. Kennedy added to his fortune by Texas oil investments and by the acquisition of real estate in New York, Palm Beach and Chicago. He purchased for $12.5 million Chicago's Merchandise Mart, which except for the Pentagon is the world's largest office building.

The list of rich Catholic families includes the Skakels of New England, who made their fortune in building materials; the Graces of New York, who earned their money in shipping and airlines; the Buckleys of Texas, who became wealthy through petroleum; the Generoso Pope clan of New York, who derived their riches from construction, cement and publishing; and the Crimmins family of New York, who struck it rich through construction and real estate.

Other moneyed Catholic families include Hoguet (banking), O'Conor (Formica), Hagerty (insurance), Shea (law), Stillman (banking), Moore (shipping), Mullen (mining), Malo (hay and feed), Robert (banking), Cudahy (meat packing), Giannini (banking), O'Neil (tire-making), Fisher (auto bodies), Miller (beer), Spaeth (beer), Busch (beer), Mann (cameras), Carey (auto rentals), Ritter (publications), Burke (department stores), Tilyou (Steeplechase of Coney Island), Hardart (restaurants), Shattuck (restaurants), Kelly (bricks), Sinatra (entertainment), Frawley (razor blades), De Menils (oil-well machinery) and Chandler (law). Some rich Catholic family names are prominent mostly in their own cities, such as Fuller, Phelan and Posi of Boston; Connelly, Forstmann, Horan, McShain, McCloskey and Murphy of Philadelphia; Burke, Clarke, Cummings, McCahey, Murphy, and Wild of Chicago; Boone, Carroll, Chatard, Cromwell, Dugan, Evans, Fenwick, Holland, Horsey, Jenkins, Lee, O'Donovan, Offutt, Shriver, Slingluff, Whelan and Walters of Baltimore; Briggs, Hart, Roche, Slattery, Tracy of Detroit; Alioto, Cameron, Cooper, De Young, Martin, Miller, Thieriot, Tobin and Tucker of San Francisco; Bezou, Carrière, Fortier, Gibbons, Henican, Nolan, Pitit, Soniat, Villère of New Orleans; and Bernet, Coakley, Fritzsche, Hauserman and O'Neill of Cleveland.

In nearly every instance, the individuals of these upper-crust families are known to be philanthropic with their money, making frequent large donations to worthy causes, especially Catholic charities. Although the Catholic Church is notoriously shy about releasing figures on contributions received each year from wills, gifts of stock, annuities, land and buildings, it is estimated to be the recipient of some $1 billion a year from these sources. No small contributors to this annual sum are the upper-middle-class Catholic families, who do not keep tight purse strings when funds are being raised for a special Catholic cause.

Among the most generous benefactors are members of the Knights of Malta, a fraternal organization, membership in which is considered a supreme honor for the Catholic layman. Membership in this society precludes for the most part anyone who is not prepared to give copiously and give promptly.

When first mentioned for nomination, a prospective Knight is expected to contribute a certain amount of money, somewhere in the neighborhood of $5,000. Meeting but once a year, they usually foregather for impressive ceremonies at St. Patrick's Cathedral in New York City, during which the Knights wear elaborate uniforms, plumes, and swords. There they attend a solemn High Mass, which is presided over by the archbishop, before going on to the big banquet, where they are invariably asked to make a handsome money donation as a way of denoting loyalty to the order and fervor for their religion.

Whatever may be said of the largesse of the big-money Catholics, the chief source of income of the Church today continues to be the Sunday-morning collection. It is this money—and no one knows how much is collected each Sunday, nor does anyone have any idea how much extra is contributed around the important Christian holidays, such as Easter and Christmas—that fleshes out the funds for current operating expenses and for capital building funds. Faced with the continued necessity of new building programs, the Church needs these regular contributions from parishioners, not only to meet current expenses and pay for buildings in actual construction, but also to pay the interest charges on mortgages taken out on Church property.

Everywhere in the United States Catholic credit is good. To keep it that way, parish priests and diocesan heads have sought, successfully, to pay off the substance of loans within the specified period of time. Every banker in America is aware of the future ability of any given parish or diocese to pay interest on money borrowed.

Although it would take an extensive statistical study to indicate precisely the ratio of church funds received from the regular contributions of the faithful to money received from income-producing securities and real estate, the data accumulated for this book convince me that the latter is relatively small in comparison. If anything, reports about Catholic "big business" in the United States (unlike those already known about the Vatican) tend to be exaggerated, deliberately or not so deliberately. Admittedly, the few annual financial statements that have so far been issued (and reported in these pages) incur a degree of doubt, since in no case has an independent outside accounting firm ever audited these statements according to generally accepted practices.

But skepticism is not a substitute for fact. And in every instance where I had an honest insight into a parish's or diocese's true financial picture I noted that the amount of money earned from investments amounted to a tiny percentage of the amount that came in from the contributions of parishioners.

American Catholics are, as a group, consistent contributors to their religion. Nearly all of these donations are made through their parishes, dioceses, special boards and agencies. At the parish level, they give regularly when the basket or plate is passed around during Mass, and they give regularly to the special monthly or semi-monthly "envelope" collections.

Additional revenue (no one knows how much) to the Catholic Church comes from the schedule of fees each parish institutes for various religious ceremonies. Given variations from one parish to another, the schedule of fees runs more or less as follows: Low Mass is officially priced for as little as one dollar, but no parishioner pays this amount. For a Mass in which a person's name is announced, the fee is a minimum of five dollars; for a Mass with one priest singing, the fee is fifteen dollars; with three priests, forty-five dollars. The charge for a funeral runs up to thirty-five dollars, and in some instances to a hundred dollars when there are as many as three priests on the altar. High Mass, which takes at least one hour, has a nominal fee of forty dollars. In many parishes bishops and pastors may keep part of the Mass stipend and farm out the actual function to an assistant or to a smaller church whose clerics do not have an abundance of requests. There are other fees, of course, for baptisms and confirmations and marriages. There is even a fee when a faithful Catholic seeks a dispensation for a mixed marriage. In this case an appeal for the permission is made to the bishop, who then sets the amount to be contributed. The sum is then divided between the bishop and Rome.*

In general, American Catholics tolerate the fee system. They give generously anyway—even to religious orders engaged in foreign missionary work. Many dioceses have a cooperative arrangement so that different orders have a chance to appeal directly to a given parish on a particular Sunday. The most important such appeal is the one made through the bishops by the Society for the Propagation of the Faith. Two fifths of the money received in this annual request is turned over to missionary dioceses in the United States itself, while the other 60 percent is sent to Rome for disbursement among various foreign missionaries. In addition, all of the Catholic societies engaged in foreign missionary work publish their own magazines or newspapers through which they make constant appeals for financial help. In spite of a strong willingness to give to international causes, American Catholics never fail to give, for example, when a strictly local appeal is made—such as money to buy coal to heat parish buildings during cold weather. The American Catholic is also a great supporter of church bazaars, raffles and other parish fund-raising projects, and is quite receptive to direct-mail appeals for money.

So where does all this money go? Short of citing specific

* The Sacred Roman Rota is a Vatican commission which has the power to declare null and void improperly contracted marriages of Catholics. Ordinarily the fee for nullifying a marriage runs to approximately $8,000. Francis J. Cardinal Brennan of Shenandoah, Pennsylvania, was the head of the Sacred Roman Rota from 1959 until his death in 1968. Another American member of the Rota is Monsignor William J. Doheny of Merrill, Wisconsin.

figures for the country, we can say that the Church gives unto others.

The money gathered from these various sources goes into operating about 18,000 parishes in the United States, into subsidizing innumerable foreign and home missions, into supporting over 785 hospitals, 420 homes for the aged and almost 240 orphanages, and into running some 13,000 schools. It is this last operation which is draining off most of the Church's money today, for education is far and away the major item in any diocese's budget. No matter where I traveled in America, I found the same thing. The churches were hurting for money because their education programs had become too expensive.

Casting aside the allegation that bishops and pastors have been falsifying their school-cost figures in their campaign to get state subsidies—allegations, by the way, that often seem to be made by people whose true objections to church "wealth" arise from their hostility to the Catholic religion itself—I came to the conclusion that if parochial schools were to be abandoned, the American Catholic Church's financial problems would almost cease to exist. The present rate of donations would be enough to support the broad spectrum of services the Church provides.

Because they realize that they will be unable to support parochial schools much longer, some of the bishops have found it expedient to issue financial reports, in order to strengthen their arguments for state subsidies. As has been pointed out here, these fiscal statements do not really give the whole picture on Catholic "wealth," either individually or collectively. Simply put, the public does not know how rich the Church is. In a book published by Random House last year (*Worldly Goods*, by James Gollin), a guess on Catholic wealth is offered by the author, who estimates it at $34.2 million, of which better than 90 percent is frozen in real estate. On the matter of

Church investments, he calculates that nearly $1.2 billion is invested in securities. Convinced that the Church's money is poorly managed by priests who he maintains are incompetent in economics, Mr. Gollin places the gross annual income of the American Catholic Church at $1.5 billion.

For that matter, there is no single high official of the clergy who has an intimate or complete knowledge concerning the wealth, income and economic structure of the American Catholic Church today. This includes the Vatican, which, contrary to what might be suspected, does not keep tabs on the myriad and complex economics of any of America's archdioceses, dioceses, religious orders or Catholic fraternal organizations. Yet these American organizations do from time to time contribute to the coffers of the Vatican, under a loosely defined quota system, some of which goes under the appellation of "gifts." What is remarkable about Catholic business is that it is not under the aegis of a single czar, not even the Pope. Most of the specific enterprises are virtually independent of each other. If there is any discipline whatever, it is a kind of self-discipline, for no one is really obliged to report to a central authority. A given archbishop may serve this function in his diocese, but only in his own rigidly defined bailiwick. Although American cardinals and bishops do visit the Pope and do present money gifts to him at given intervals, they are not obliged to give an accounting or a financial report of the various business enterprises in their jurisdictions. In fact, it has been long suspected —and I uncovered any number of such instances—that within an archdiocese, various parish priests often elect to keep the exact state of their finances, their earnings and their revenue to themselves, so that the annual contribution to the chancery can be kept to the minimum. Not only do the parishes play this game, but the dioceses themselves sometimes engage in a similar kind of "deception" with their immediate superiors.

Usually when a diocese is facing serious money problems, a bishop or archbishop will be told the full state of affairs. But when things are on a sound financial basis, there may be sly maneuvers to "misinform" the next ranking official. A local pastor will rationalize his close-mouthedness by telling himself that the money will be put to better use in his own backyard than in the chancery or the already affluent Vatican. Many parish priests were queried about this matter and some of them admitted, "We try to get away with what we can when it comes to our limited funds and the quotas."

To understand how the parish quota system functions, let us look at a specific example. There are variations, of course, but the following runs true for all U.S. parishes:

In a memorandum entitled "Cathedraticum Quotas 1969," one American bishop imposed three different kinds of quotas on each of his parishes, though obviously the figures varied from parish to parish. The memo explained that the tax (quota) was "now due and payable at the chancery," said money to be used to support the bishop's house, the chancery, the matrimonial tribunal, the central administration of the diocese, and the various organizations of regional or national scope to which the diocese was expected to contribute.

> Because of the great increase in these responsibilities in recent years and anticipated expenses this year [the directive read], it has become necessary to increase the Cathedraticum quotas. The following are a few of the items involved in this increase: (1) Support of the state Catholic Conference from approximately $800 biennially to approximately $8,000 per year; (2) Support of the National Conference of Catholic Bishops and the U.S. Catholic Conference from approximately $2,500 per year to $7,200 per year; (3) Personnel Director salary and expenses approximately $5,000 per year; (4) Diocesan

Board of Education approximately $1,000 per year, and (5) Diocesan Pastoral Council approximately $1,000 per year.

After reviewing these matters and examining the chancery and other budgets, the Assembly of Priests Cathedraticum Committee agreed that it was realistic to establish a Cathedraticum quota for 1969 of $100,000. This is an increase of approximately 20 percent. It is interesting to note that this would be slightly less than 1 percent of total parish income as indicated by the annual reports.

Also listing a Seminary Fund quota and a Newman Apostolate quota, the memo explained that the total amount of the three quotas came to approximately $355,000 whereas when the undersigned bishop came to the diocese several years earlier the parish assessments for the Seminary Fund and the Cathedraticum alone totaled $380,000. Appended was a list of the parishes and the specific assessments for each. The heaviest assessments for the biggest city in the parish were $1,900 for the Cathedraticum, $3,230 for the Seminary Fund, and $1,615 for the Newman Apostolate, whereas the same quotas for the smallest parish were $60, $100 and $50 respectively.

What happens if a pastor disagrees with the quotas that are ascribed to him by his bishop? Squabbles of this kind take place all the time, but the outside world rarely, if ever, hears about them.

An exception was the case of Monsignor J. Stanley Ormsby, pastor of Our Lady of the Rosary Church in Niagara Falls, New York, who in 1968 objected to a $120,000 levy imposed on his church by Bishop James A. McNulty of the Buffalo Diocese. Monsignor Ormsby's church had recently completed payments on a $150,000 mortgage, and he did not believe that his 820 low-income-family parishioners could afford an additional burden. He noted that during a diocesan development fund campaign between 1964 and 1967 his church had been assessed $600 per week, but that his parishioners could come up with only about $100 a week. He also noted that mandatory delivery of the diocesan newspaper, *The Magnificat*, was an added financial strain. Each member of his church was supposed to have paid five dollars a year for a subscription, but fewer than a hundred did; as a result, his church had to pay $300 a month to make up the difference. Monsignor Ormsby made it clear that he was not opposed to Bishop McNulty *per se* but rather to a system in which "autocratically and dictatorially debts are levied on a parish without any consultation or agreement—a system which should be altered." Despite his protests, which were duly reported in the press, Monsignor Ormsby ultimately recanted and agreed to pay the assessment.

Obscuring the Church's overall financial picture is the autonomy of its units. But every five years a bishop must appear in person before the Pope to give a report of his work and his diocese. These reports, however, need not contain detailed financial data. It is known that insofar as the American Catholic Church is concerned, the Vatican does not keep any kind of overall balance sheet. As one high-ranking cleric in the Midwest put it, "From a Wall Street point of view, I guess you'd say that Catholic finances are one big mess. And maybe they are. But we are not in this business to grow rich."

On the other hand, the Vatican will intrude in the business affairs of an American cleric when something goes utterly wrong. There is the case of one bishop several years ago who lost a large sum, most of it diocesan funds and the rest his personal money, when he made some bad investments in a mining deal. Quietly the Vatican stepped in and "removed" him. Instead of assigning the man to another part of the United States or kicking him upstairs by placing him in an obscure post inside the Vatican, the Pope kept him on as titular head of the diocese and appointed another high churchman to take over actual control as coadjutor. These matters are usually taken care of without the knowledge of local parishioners, since the more militant ones would not brook direct interference from Rome.

There is probably not a single practicing adult Catholic in the United States today who has not pondered the Vatican with a bit of suspicion. Inevitably, an American Catholic asks himself: How much money contributed by America's Catholic faithful gets sent to Rome each year? And what happens to this money?

Guesses range all the way from a mere million dollars to several billion. The truth, of course, would have to lie somewhere in between. The largest amount of money that goes to Rome from the United States comes from the annual Peter's Pence collection which is made in all churches at the end of June. The day of the collection is usually June 29, and it involves every diocese all over the globe. The total sum that comes from Peter's Pence, presumably to be used for the support of the works of the Holy See, is said to be $1.5 million. Not many experts place much stock in this figure, however. The Peter's Pence collection in the United States alone is close to $6 million, according to calculations made for this book.

The origin of Peter's Pence has been traced as far back as the year 787, when it was first collected in England. It remained a fixed obligation down to the time of King Henry VIII, in the early part of the sixteenth century. Then it spread to other northern lands. Still other countries adopted Peter's Pence and for centuries it persisted in many places. Existing records in Portugal, Poland and certain of the Italian states do not make clear which revenues derived from Peter's Pence and which from the feudal tribute, the price of papal protection. The Reformation brought an end to Peter's Pence temporarily, and it did not reappear until the middle of the nineteenth century, during the reign of Pope Pius IX—first in France, then in Austria and Germany, later in Ireland. In the United States, Peter's Pence was revived in 1868 in Baltimore when the Second Plenary Council decided to take up a collection in American churches for the Pope once a year. At the turn of the century, France was the principal contributor to Peter's Pence, but now first place has been taken over by the American Catholic Church. The money is sent each year through the Apostolic Delegate's Office in Washington, and the Pope is accountable to no one as to how he administers these funds.

In addition to Peter's Pence, Rome requires of the United States what are called "supplementi," or additional contributions. These are usually percentages of other collections that are taken throughout the year, and they are all managed by the American Board of Catholic Missions. This Board distributes between 40 and 60 percent of these collected monies to various parts of the United States (principally the South and the Southwest) and funnels a certain percentage to the Vatican.

One of these annual mission collections is for the Society for the Propagation of the Faith, and the contributions from all sources around the world come to a total of about $30 million each year, $6.5–7 million of which comes from the United States and all of which goes to Rome. Other collections are those for the Catholic Relief and Bishop Relief and the Catholic Near East Society.

Over and above these funds and percentages that are forwarded to Rome are the so-called Ad Limina visitations by the various bishops and the offerings to Rome for quinquennial faculties. Various "taxes" are levied on American bishops, who must pay at least one visit to the Pope every five years, at which time they are expected to present a donation to the Pope. The average gift ranges between $2,000 and $3,000, but a few archbishops from some of the richer American jurisdictions will go as high as $5,000.

Taking into account the Ad Limina visitations, the annual Peter's Pence contribution and the "supplementi," it is estimated that the 123 dioceses in the United States give a total of about $15 million a year to Rome. Mention should be made here that the Vatican practices a rigid policy of never sending any of this money back to the United States for charitable purposes, no matter how pressing the need, for the view of the hierarchy in Rome is that the United States is the richest country in the world and can take care of itself. The Pope has been known to send money to "disaster areas"—but so far never to the United States.

To understand better how the economics of American Catholicism is set up in terms of the Vatican, one must understand the degree of local autonomy in the operation of the Church. Though papal authorization is present in matters of canon law, the Vatican does not make its presence felt in how a parish raises funds for a new building. A look, therefore, at the governing machinery is in order at this point.

The cardinals, who are the advisers and executive assistants of the Pope, no matter where they are stationed in the world, hold positions somewhat akin to a vice-president in a corporation. It is at the rank below cardinal that the key work is done, for the archbishops and bishops rule over the more than 1,300 dioceses in the world, each of which consists of a number of parishes in a specific geographical area.

The backbone of the Roman Catholic Church is the bishops, of whom there are between 163 and 165 in the United States. A resident bishop has complete power in his jurisdiction. Representing the Church in his area, he owns in trust or controls the real property of the Church, and he must keep all income under supervision. Although he has a position of independent authority, every bishop toes the approved Vatican line. He is obliged to visit every one of his churches at least once a year and every foundation in his area once every three years. Apart from rendering an accounting of his activities to the Pope every five years, he must also be in constant communication with his Washington superior, the Apostolic Delegate, who holds a position comparable to that of a staff officer of the Holy See.

Because of the character and training of the bishop himself and the peculiarities of his diocese, the operating efficiency of each diocese varies greatly. Since the central structure of the Church is authoritarian and the role of the layman is completely passive, the bishop dominates the financial machinery. Dioceses are not in any manner compelled to conform to a common norm, so that each bishop does what he wants in the way that he wants within his area. Since many of the dioceses in the United States are staffed by priests who do not have the capacity or aptitude for administration or the handling of money matters, the bishop is ultimately the one who has to deal with the mundane intricacies of fiscal matters. In a broad sense, therefore, the bishop is the general manager of a diocese. And in carrying out his job he has a team of workers under him, such as auxiliary bishops, monsignors and parish priests, who lend their respective talents to an organization whose problems rival those of any financial institution in America.

Multiply a given diocesan complex dozens and dozens of times, and one begins to understand just how big the Roman Catholic Church operation in the United States is. It is estimated (by Catholic sources) that the total operating expenditures of all the dioceses surpass a total of $420 million a year. No other organization in North America, religious or secular, attempts such a broad operation.

Yet despite the vastness and complexity of this financial organization, there is no one overall boss. It can safely be said that as far as money matters are concerned, every archdiocese and diocese is autonomous. Each bishop shepherds his own flock and does not interfere in the financial affairs of other bishops.

One of the largest dioceses in the world—and the biggest in North America—is the Chicago Archdiocese. It contains more than two million persons in 439 parishes, with 2,700 priests and 8,600 nuns. Operating an educational system that includes nine seminaries, six universities and colleges, eighty-eight high schools, 426 elementary schools and a student population of better than 350,000, the Chicago Archdiocese also administers twenty-one general hospitals, many homes for the aged, a number of orphanages, nursing schools and sanatoriums.

Like every other diocese in the United States and Canada, Chicago is not in day-to-day touch with the Vatican for guidance on fiscal matters. The archdiocese raises its own funds, meets its own business obligations, works out its own building program and administers its own money. The Chicago Archdiocese is a corporation sole (as explained in Chapter 6); everything it owns or owes is in the name of the Chicago Archbishop (John Cardinal Cody has been archbishop since 1965). In lending money to its parishes, the archdiocese, which receives the prime interest rate from banks, charges anywhere from one-quarter to one-half percent above the prime rate. In effect, therefore, the archdiocese acts as a central bank for its parishes. On the other hand, parishes that are in good financial shape are expected, and sometimes forced, to lend money to the chancery so that the bishop can in turn use the money for loans to parishes that require it. When a given parish borrows money to build another church or school—the average loan is about $600,000—the money has to be repaid with interest within a decade.

How this operates is graphically shown in a letter that the bishop of one Midwestern jurisdiction sent out to his parishes in September 1969. Except for a few minor deletions to disguise the location, the confidential letter is printed exactly as circulated.

At the request of our Business Office I wish to discuss with you our central Diocesan Financing Program. It seems urgent that I should ask for your fullest participation in this program at this time for the mutual welfare of all of our parishes.

This program tries to provide financing for all parishes in the diocese at the best possible rates by utilizing the surplus funds of parishes and the overall credit rating of the diocese, which has been able to borrow at prime rates not always available to parishes. Thus we have been able to assist in the development of many parish projects, while at the same time providing a reasonable return on surplus funds in a safe investment.

As you probably know, the cost of borrowings has now reached rates not dreamed of a few short months ago. During the past 18 months the "prime rate" interest charged by banks has risen from 5½ per cent to 8½ per cent. Despite this 3 point rise, or 55 per cent increase in the cost of credit, we have been able to maintain a 5½ per cent rate on demand loans to our parishes since April 1, 1968. However, after recent evaluation of our program it became obvious that continued extension of credit at this rate would be financially impossible.

Accordingly, the matter was reviewed by the Board of Diocesan Consultors recently and it was decided that the rate charged to parishes must be increased to 6 per cent, effective July 1, 1969, with an understanding that the matter be reviewed again before October to determine whether such rate should continue to apply.

Although the 6 per cent rate is the highest ever charged on loans to our parishes, the cost of such credit is substantially lower than that available to the nation's largest corporations. According to information recently published in financial journals, the rate of interest being paid by a number of ——'s largest corporations is 8¾ per cent. In view of these conditions, it would appear that our financial program has been reasonably successful toward minimizing and stabilizing the cost of credit to our parishes. The fact that the money market has experienced a 3 point rise during a period when our charges have risen only ½ point is a good example of its benefits and effectiveness.

Simultaneous with review of our lending program, the matter of our parish investment program was reviewed and a decision made to pay a higher rate of return. Effective July 1, 1969, the rate for short term deposits will be 5 per cent, and for long term 5½ per cent. Such interest is computed by the day and compounded quarterly if left on deposit. By applying such mechanics, the rate of return actually exceeds the fixed annual rate and without risk of interest loss if withdrawal should become necessary before the close of a quarter.

In view of these procedures and beneficial policies, I expect that all parishes will make every effort to cooperate and participate in the program. For those who have borrowed through the diocese, I urge you to establish a plan for systematic and monthly payment of principal and prompt payment of interest.

I urgently ask those who have surplus funds to deposit them with the Business Office on either a short or long term basis. May I suggest that you check to see how large a bank balance you are carrying from month to month to see whether perhaps you should place some funds on investment at least for a short term. This is not only a means for exercising sound business practices, but a most important way of demonstrating collegial support of the Church.

With sentiments of gratitude for your cooperation and begging God's blessings upon our mutual efforts, I remain
Sincerely yours in Christ,

Whenever appeals for money are made by Catholic officials, the question of the Church's "wealth" raises its ugly head. Inevitably, mention is made of the Church's real-estate holdings. It bothers some people that the Roman Catholic Church in the United States possesses more property than any one private organization. In Washington, D.C., for example (just to cite one city), the Church owns nearly 60 percent of all tax-exempt land aside from that held by the federal agencies. The real estate in Washington is already three times the size of the whole of Vatican City.

As sometimes happens with certain organizations directly involved in business affairs, the Catholic Church has developed its own "style." For the most part Catholic officials show a predilection for real estate. A fact of Catholic business life, corroborated recently in a public statement by Thomas J. Gibbons, a lay official of the New York Catholic Conference, is that the American Catholic Church ranks second only to the United States government in total annual purchases of real estate. A former Roman Catholic priest from the Far West who had served in the chancery of a major archdiocese and been personally close to the archbishop explained the thinking of his superior with regard to the wisdom of acquiring real estate as opposed to engaging in any other kind of investment. He reported his archbishop as saying that "if one buys big acreages and then sells them by the lot, your money grows like wild wheat." The archbishop believed that land investments, unlike stock-market securities, are a hedge against inflation. His thinking was based on the following premises: that the supply of land is fixed, while the demand grows constantly; that wealthy corporations today are finding the countryside more to their liking and so are moving from the city (and going with them are middle-class families with sufficient money for investments); that there is an increasing interest in the outdoors and in recreation by families whose business keeps them in the city but whose affluence permits them to journey to the countryside on weekends. Thus this particular archbishop, along with other important Catholic officials throughout the country, is convinced of the wisdom of stock-piling land.

It is hard to deduce just where this American Catholic Church appetite for real estate comes from. Perhaps from the Vatican. For the Vatican has over the centuries been strongly disposed to land acquisitions. Yet other Catholic dioceses in other parts of the world have not seemed to follow the Vatican's leadership in this regard, whereas the American Church has even surpassed the Vatican in total landholdings. Perhaps the predilection came from the original Catholic clergymen in America's Colonial period who made good at the outset by acquiring land. And perhaps it has simply to do with the fact that the United States is a business society where the interests of business take precedence over those of society as a whole. The American attitude, by and large, is to get richer and then get richer.

It has frequently been observed, and not without substance, that going broke is one of the worst crimes one can commit in the American capitalist society. There is no faster way to lose the respect of your fellow man in the United States than to lose your money. The Church, like most other institutions, has fallen into this ethos. One would almost think that by this time still another Commandment would have been added to the already established Decalogue—"Thou shalt not go broke."

Still, as we all know, "Money talks!" That is an expression one hears all over the United States, a nation that displays a reverence for the Almighty Dollar. Success in America is often equated with business achievement, and this notion will no doubt go on right into the "brave new world" of the Year X.

One can almost be sure that the Catholic Church, the Christian churches, will follow suit. It seems almost ironic that on the one hand, Christianity was born of a poor man who preached poverty and practiced it for 33 years. Yet, on the other hand, a Rip Van Winkle from an earlier century would be flabbergasted today were he to return to the world of the 1970s and see the churches, Catholic and Protestant alike, with their overwhelming ostentation of material success. And it is no wonder, for the business syndrome is part of the bone and sinew that go to make up America and its religions. The Catholic religion is no small exception. Somewhere along the line the Church seems to have been infused with a compulsive motivation to harvest as much money as the variety of methods will allow.

I am reminded of Supreme Court Justice William O. Douglas' story of a time when he was flying in a plane that was hit by lightning. As the aircraft pitched precariously, he related, nobody among the passengers knew what to do. "Do something religious," a little lady across the aisle suggested. "So I did," said Justice Douglas. "I took up a collection." And that inscrutable observer from England, Malcolm Muggeridge, was reported in the Denver *Post* to have made his personal observation about religion in America: "Religion is little more than an efficiently run business enterprise. I actually heard one clergyman refer to his church as 'my plant.'"

When one figures the worth of all the Catholic churches, elementary schools, high schools, universities, rectories, convents, orphanages, homes for the aged and hospitals, not to mention uncounted empty real-estate tracts, one can understand why there are many groups and private individuals who are apprehensive about "the wealth of the Catholic Church." Small wonder that one anti-Catholic pamphlet shrieks: "The Catholic Church is the fourth richest corporation in the United States."

Before I set out to do the research on this book, I too had

been awed by the "wealth" of the Church. But I found that although the American Catholic Church does indeed possess substantial visible riches, it does not have cash. Essentially, the Church is land rich but money poor. The bulk of its "wealth" today is tied up in school buildings, hospitals and other buildings that serve religious, educational and charitable purposes. Far from being financial assets to the Church, these structures drain much, if not all, of the cash the Church takes in, especially the money from the offerings of the faithful, which generally is earmarked for internal operating expenses. There are no figures available for any year which show how much is contributed to American parishes, but most experts would put the amount at no less than $2 billion a year. Yet nearly every parish and church in the United States has deepening financial troubles and is strapped for cash. And there are many bishops and pastors who are running scared.

So here we touch on the edge of the problem, which the bishops' silence has indeed aggravated. Moneywise, the American Catholic Church is in a bad fix. Many of the dioceses are on the brink of bankruptcy, and there is growing doubt whether the Church can in the foreseeable future do anything to greatly improve its position. These are the cold facts about the "richness" of the American Catholic Church today. Some may pooh-pooh them; some may not. But there they are.

12

MEANWHILE, BACK AT THE VATICAN . . .

The way to stop financial joy-riding is to arrest the chauffeur, not the automobile.—WOODROW WILSON

SEVERAL YEARS AGO, while on a visit to downtown Rome, Pope Paul VI found himself in danger when an overenthusiastic crowd broke through police lines and began to push toward him. For a short time it appeared that the Pontiff would be badly trampled. Then suddenly, from out of nowhere, a brawny priest came to the Pope's rescue. Using his buffalo-wide shoulders and wielding elbows like pistons, he cleaved a passage for the Pontiff, saving him from what appeared to be certain injury. Later, back inside the Vatican, Pope Paul called the big cleric, an American from Cicero, Illinois, to his office and thanked him personally. So much had the oversized Yank impressed His Holiness with his herculean performance that he was appointed to serve as the Pope's personal bodyguard—something no Pope had ever had before.

Known affectionately inside the Leonine Walls as "the Gorilla," the Pope's bodyguard is forty-nine-year-old Bishop Paul Marcinkus. Bishop Marcinkus does not carry firearms, but he has a highly educated pair of fists and it is unanimously agreed that Paul Marcinkus is a good man not to tangle with. He has shielded Pope Paul during his foreign trips to India, the Middle East, the United States, Portugal, Turkey, Colombia, Switzerland and the Far East and also on visits in various parts of Italy.

But Bishop Marcinkus has another, less conspicuous job in the office of the Vatican's Secretariat of State. He is in executive control of the Vatican's Institute for Religious Works, a post that makes him responsible for handling the investment of hundreds of millions of dollars belonging to Roman Catholic orders and charities in all parts of the world. The Institute also manages the foreign portion of the Holy See's substantial securities portfolio. Most of the investments the Vatican has outside Italy are American, and it is estimated that Bishop Marcinkus watches over approximately $2 billion worth of equity shares quoted on Wall Street. The Yankee prelate, who has admitted to friends that he "is not very good at figures," subscribes to the dictum that what is good for General Motors is also good for the Vatican. But the Vatican's investments go far beyond shareholdings. Its total financial activity is a much bigger operation and is not under the American bishop-banker's supervision.

While the American Catholic Church is going through some tough times, prosperity booms behind the Leonine Walls. But trying to view the business operation of the sanctum sanctorum of Catholicism's world headquarters is like looking through a toy kaleidoscope. With each turn the total picture and pattern change, while the shapes and the colors of the individual pieces stay the same. As one of the greatest fiscal powers in the world, the Vatican, like Rome, was not built in a day. And its wealth was not accumulated overnight. In the pursuit of profit, the Vatican flexes its economic muscles and assembles all its best punches to knock down anything that threatens to kayo the basic solvency of its operations.

Some of the credit for the Vatican's success in becoming an economic empire can be attributed to the tax-free benefits of the Lateran Pact of 1929, which also provided Pope Pius XI with a lump sum of approximately $90 million. This windfall came at a time when the Vatican found itself in serious financial straits. Not many people were or are aware that the Vatican, following the end of the First World War, had come very close to bankruptcy. In 1919 Pope Benedict VI discreetly but unsuccessfully tried to negotiate a loan of about $1 million in the United States. As luck would have it, that was the year the Knights of Columbus had picked for a pilgrimage to Rome, and they brought to the Pope a gift of $250,000. That the Vatican was almost broke and that they had come to its rescue was something the visiting delegates could not have known.

When Pope Benedict died in 1922, the Vatican still had money troubles. Despite the aid from the Knights of Columbus, finances had skidded badly. If Pope Benedict had been a flop as a manager of the Church's money, his successor, Pope Pius XI, was possibly even worse. In 1928 Pope Pius appointed Monsignor Dominique Mariani as the secretary of a cardinals' committee to manage the Holy See's property. Ordered to take an inventory, Monsignor Mariani conducted the first audit in the Church's history. From this he learned that the Vatican's expenses in a given day generally came to $5,000. He also came up with the disturbing disclosure that the Vatican was virtually down to the last dollar. Monsignor Mariani tried to apply a tourniquet to papal spending and instituted some penny-pinching practices, but with no notable success. If the Vatican was to solve its money problem help was needed from the outside. And help did come. In 1928 George

Cardinal Mundelein, Archbishop of the Chicago Archdiocese, having been taken into the Pope's confidence, floated a loan of $1.5 million through twenty-year bonds backed by several million dollars' worth of Church property in Chicago.

That loan put the Vatican back on its feet. But it was the $90 million from the 1929 Lateran Pact that really swung the pendulum in the other direction. Nowadays the Vatican ledgers are written in black ink, and much of the credit belongs to a onetime architect, Bernardino Nogara, who, after being entrusted by the Pope to administer the vast sum of Lateran money, demonstrated his financial genius by building an empire. Mr. Nogara, apparently driven by deep religious motivations, became the Pope's "secret weapon." For all intents and purposes, this man turned out to be, in the words of one cardinal, "the best thing that has happened to the Vatican since Our Lord Jesus Christ."

As administrator of pontifical funds, he answered to no one, not even to the committee of three cardinals which, theoretically, supervised his activities. Nor did Pope Pius have any specific idea as to what, if anything, Mr. Nogara was doing with the $90 million. In actual fact, the Vatican's financial fox was carrying out his own pet theory—that in matters of dollars and sense *tempus* must not be allowed to *fugit*.

Given the kind of leeway that would doubtless be the envy of many large-company executives, Mr. Nogara abided by a self-imposed rule that the Vatican's investment program should not be hampered by religious considerations. He undertook a world investment policy that caused the initial capital to soar. When he died, late in 1958, he left behind a "methodology" that is followed religiously by his successors, who continue to churn out profits.

As perhaps the world's largest business organization, the Vatican has realizable assets roughly equal to the official gold and foreign-exchange reserves of France. Today the Vatican is firmly entrenched in numerous companies engaged in real estate, plastics, electronics, steel manufacturing, cement, textiles, chemicals, food products and construction. It is one of Italy's largest bankers and owns several big Italian insurance companies. Having penetrated into almost every sector of Italian economy and become involved in business enterprises in other parts of the world, especially the United States and Canada, the world's smallest sovereign domain is a formidable international financial power with a corporate wealth that is in excess of $20 billion.

Many of the stocks owned by the Vatican in Italy are held through front companies such as banks, special credit institutions and insurance companies. The Vatican's Italian portfolio alone comes to approximately one fifteenth of the total number of shares quoted on the ten Italian stock exchanges.

This fact, and some alleged tax-evasion practices, recently put the Vatican's stock-market operation into the public limelight. Back in 1963 Premier Giovanni Leone's caretaker Cabinet, in an exchange of diplomatic notes with the state of Vatican City, agreed that a new dividend tax that went into effect that year was not to be applied to the investment profits of the Vatican. The Minister of Finance Mario Martinelli sent a circular letter to the tax-collection agencies advising them of the secret deal which had been made with the Vatican. When a new Finance Minister, Roberto Tremelloni, took over he refused to abide by the agreement. For several months after that, the new Premier, Aldo Moro, tried to affect a compromise. He asked the Vatican to submit a statement of its holdings as a prelude to obtaining an exemption. But the Vatican Secretary of State refused, claiming that one sovereign state does not tell another the details of its finances. So Premier Moro, trying to be a good referee, resorted to an old fighter's trick—he "held back and waited for the clock to run out." That almost worked.

In mid-1964 a new Minister of the Treasury, Giovanni Pieraccini, also declined to ratify the Vatican's exemption. That was a year when the business barometer showed its low opinion of the Italian economy, and the Vatican made capital of this temporary adversity by threatening to dump on the stock market several hundred million dollars' worth of shares. If it had carried out this bluff, it would have depressed the market at a time when to do so might have inflicted some deep wounds on the economy. But to the rescue of the Vatican and Premier Moro came a hastily formed stock-exchange group which lobbied successfully, with a modicum of arm-twisting.

Typical of Italian politics, some kind of deal was made in October 1964 whereby the Moro Cabinet sponsored a parliamentary bill, known as Bill 1773, formalizing the dividend-tax exemption for the Vatican that had been agreed upon in the diplomatic notes in 1963. After going through the appropriate parliamentary committee, the bill was to go to Parliament for a vote. This did not happen. Nor did anybody seem to be in any kind of hurry. The matter lay dormant for several years, the while the Vatican paid no taxes on its stock holdings.

Then early in 1967 the bottom fell out again. The leftist Rome weekly *L'Espresso* wanted to know why the "biggest tax evader in postwar Italy" was not paying levies on its income like other companies. And Finance Minister Luigi Preti made an unusual disclosure for an Italian official. He told the Senate that the Vatican had received $5.22 million in Italian dividends in 1965 and that it should have paid $1.6 million in taxes that year. In response to this, sources close to Pope Paul VI cited the Lateran Treaty of 1929, which recognized the Vatican as a sovereign independent state and exempted it from Italian taxation. And the Vatican's unofficial newspaper declared that the money was, in any case, "holy money, entirely earmarked for charity."

In July 1968 a new Cabinet made it known that the Vatican would have to pay its tax arrears. Premier Leone declared in a state-of-the-nation message that rather than grant a new tax exemption at the end of 1968, the government intended to let the exemption drop and not seek parliamentary ratification for new exemptions.

Church officials immediately issued a protest through the Holy See's press office. A spokesman noted that the Vatican contributed heavily to Italy's income with its investments and tourist attractions. Moreover, he said, several other countries, including the United States, were giving the Roman Catholic Church tax exemptions because of its special nature and work. He reaffirmed the view that the taxing of the Holy See's income would take away money destined for religious and social-work projects.

In the end, however, the Vatican capitulated.

Late in 1968 the Vatican let it be known that it would pay taxes on its Italian stock earnings. Explaining that it did not have funds on hand to meet such a large bill immediately, the Vatican asked permission to meet the tax in installments. The Holy See requested a statement from the Italian government as to how much would have to be paid. Apparently this has not been provided, for no figures were ever made public. On the basis of Finance Minister Preti's estimate that the Vatican should have paid $1.6 million taxes in 1965, it would appear that it is $14.4 million in arrears in taxes on its security holdings in Italy for the years 1963–1971.

This sort of behind-the-scenes activity is typical of the way the Vatican keeps its financial operations behind a veil of obscurity, even at a time when business and economics have become an area of avid interest. Although the Vatican has been successful in keeping its money matters to itself most of the time, there was an exception on the occasion when Pope John needed to pay some big bills that had accrued from the Ecumenical Council and was compelled to sell $4.5 million in gold to the United States government. (This sum of money did not underwrite the Vatican's total expenditure for the Council, which came to a total of better than $20 million; miscellaneous costs alone reached $7.2 million.)

Apart from that item, which did get newspaper attention, little or nothing is reported on the Vatican's financial affairs. Generally ignored is the fact that the Vatican has an interest in a wide variety of companies which engage in the making of wool, silk, buttons, sugar, dynamite, ready-to-wear garments, toilet paper, spaghetti and pharmaceuticals, among other things. One Vatican company even manufactures an oral birth-control pill. The last-named product, marketed under the name "Luteolas," sells in every pharmacy in Italy at $1.90 for a supply of twenty. Although Pope Paul condemned the use of contraception in his historic "Humanae Vitae" encyclical—a document that brought on a swell of rejection from Catholics, both laymen and clergy, and evident cracks in the façade of Roman Catholic unity*—the Vatican-owned Istituto Farmacologico Serono of Rome never stopped manufacturing and distributing Luteolas.

The Serono company has been in the drug-making business since 1906, when it was known as Istituto Nazionale Medico Farmacologico. During the 1930s it began to undergo considerable financial difficulties, and it was then that Vatican finan-

* To American Catholics not used to inner-Vatican politics, it must come as a shock to learn that behind the papal throne the dirty game of politics is frequently played. Political maneuvering is practiced by the Curia strong men, most of whom are the septuagenarian Italian cardinals whose Catholicism, often cast in a medieval mold, is not above the fine Italian art of conspiracy. No matter how scandalous these intrigues would be if known to the outside, the orthodox cardinals do not hesitate to badger the Pope. Such was the case when the liberal majority inside the Vatican wanted the question of the use of contraception left up to the conscience of the individual, as did Pope Paul himself, but the curial structure finally pressured the Pontiff into accepting the views of the minority on birth control and to issuing his now controversial edict condemning contraception.

cier Nogara decided to step in with papal funds. Today Serono, which manufactures and sells several hundred other pharmaceutical products besides the Pill (including a product called Pergonal, which increases fertility), has a payroll of some 250 people who work in a modern, automated plant. The thriving drug company, with a capitalization of $1.4 million, shows an annual profit of about $170,000, according to Prince Giulio Pacelli, a nephew of the late Pope Pius XII, who is chairman of the Serono board of directors.

Another Vatican-controlled company is the SNIA-Viscosa Company of Milan, which produces more than 70 percent of Italy's artificial and synthetic fibers. Though not directly owned by the Vatican, the company itself is tied to two Vatican-owned companies—the CISA-Viscosa Company, which produces viscose fibers and rayon, and the Saici Company, which manufactures cellulose and which holds considerable stock in a cotton plant, Cotonificio Veneziano.

One of the companies—this one fully Vatican-owned—with the longest tentacles is Italgas, which controls the subsidiary gas companies in thirty-six Italian cities (including Rome, Venice, Florence and Turin). With a capital of nearly $60 million, Italgas also controls a number of companies that deal in tar, iron ore, coke for steel mills, distillates, drinking water, gas stoves, gas appliances and industrial ovens. The Vatican also owns two spaghetti factories—one in Florence and one in Rome. The Rome company, Molini Pantanella, boxes a hundred different types of pasta from *abissini* to *zite*. As a profitable sideline, Pantanella also produces holiday cakes and an assortment of fifty-two different types of cookies in its modern, air-conditioned plant.

Another company in which the Vatican has a heavy participation is the Italcementi Company. It accounts for 32 percent of the total cement production of Italy, the world's sixth-largest producer of that product, and has an annual gross income of approximately $65 million. This same company owned a financial institution known as Italmobiliare. During 1967 eight banks in Italy bought by Italmobiliare merged to give life to the new Istituto Bancario Italiano (I.B.I.), which now claims reserves of close to $9 million and shows an annual profit of over a half million. The I.B.I. combine is headed by Carlo Pesenti, also director general of Italcementi. Mr. Pesenti, who is one of Italy's most knowledgeable bankers and is considered one of the Vatican's most valuable "men of trust," bought the eight banks one at a time over a five-year span, in what some economic observers consider one of the most brilliant financial maneuvers in Italy's recent economic history.

Another bank that is owned outright by the Vatican is the Banco di Santo Spirito, one of the oldest banks in the world. Founded by Pope Paul V in 1605, the Banco di Santo Spirito has a social capital set at $12.8 million and total deposits that are over $700 million. Foremost among the Vatican-owned banks in Italy, however, is the Banco Ambrosiano in Milan; it has a capital of $6.2 million and reports a profit of over $1 million every year. Several years ago the Banco Ambrosiano bought interests in three foreign fiscal organizations—two banks in Luxembourg and one in Switzerland. It is known that the Vatican maintains large deposits in several numbered Swiss bank accounts, although some Vatican money is kept in American banks too. The Swiss accounts provide the Vatican with an anonymity that can count for a lot in certain types of transactions. Unlike American banks, Swiss banks can and often do act as stockbrokers, and they hold large numbers of securities belonging to clients but not in the clients' names.

That the Vatican has a nice slice of Italy's economic pie can also be seen in the infrequently publicized activities of the special credit institutes. Of the some 180 medium- and long-term special credit institutions in Italy, at least a third contain a flow of pontifical funds. Long-term loans indeed constitute a highly important source of financing for new expansion programs, and in this respect Vatican money has done much to shore up small and medium-sized businesses, a factor that has served the cause of capitalism in the balanced growth of Italy's postwar economy. These credit institutes serve particular sectors of the economy—i.e., credit for industry, public works and public utilities, real estate and housing, agriculture, hotels, tourism, motion pictures and the like. Some of these organizations operate on a national scale, while others are limited to individual regions. Together with the Italian banks, the special credit institutes are the major source of new capital.

To keep a going concern going money has to be spent in large amounts. The Vatican is no exception. With a payroll that comes to nearly $8 million a year, the Vatican has annual expenditures that would stagger any large-scale conglomerate. Informed Vatican observers conservatively estimate that the Pope has total annual operating expenses that exceed $20 million and probably approach $30 million. The Vatican's huge palace, offices and residential buildings and grounds must be maintained. An extensive diplomatic corps, which includes papal "ambassadors" in over eighty countries, must have funds. A fleet of sixty automobiles must be kept in running order. The maintenance of St. Peter's Basilica and St. Peter's Square alone runs to approximately $2,000 a day. A powerful radio station must be operated; a daily newspaper (with few ads—it loses $2 million a year!) must be printed six days a week. A huge staff from cardinals down to the ushers must be paid—not to mention Latinists, electricians, throne bearers, lawyers, librarians and myriads of others who provide their services inside and outside the Leonine Walls.

Even though it is unharassed by unions, the Vatican is today beset with labor problems. In May 1970 Pope Paul granted a 10 percent pay increase across the board to some three thousand employees and nine hundred pensioners. This included everyone who works at the Vatican except the cardinals (the Pope himself does not receive a salary). The raise was the second hike in eighteen months, there having been only one other pay increase prior to that, a 100 percent jump granted by Pope John in 1959 to those workers who were in the lowest income bracket.

Burdened with rising costs, Pope Paul in September 1970 disbanded all his armed and uniformed military units except the halberd-wielding Swiss Guards. The retrenchment of the pontifical military establishment, which affected more than six hundred officers and men, came after a period of strained labor relations. The blue-uniformed gendarmes had staged a four-day protest a few weeks before, refusing to collect their monthly paychecks because of the Vatican's failure to make the May salary increase retroactive.

The man currently responsible for the Vatican's finances is the Pope's "minister of finance," Egidio Cardinal Vagnozzi, who for nine years had served as the Apostolic Delegate to the United States. An admirer of the "American way of doing things," Cardinal Vagnozzi is, as I have said earlier, a close observer of the American economy. Today Cardinal Vagnozzi remains as inconspicuous as possible—and in that sense characteristic of the Vatican's business outlook.

Inasmuch as the Vatican's complex business operations have been wrapped in silence, the public image of the Roman Catholic Church remains by and large ecclesiastical. But, as I have shown here and in my previous book, the Vatican's leaders and financial advisers have carved a niche for the Papacy in the world of big business.

Aware of its growing reputation as a capitalist power in Italy, the Vatican is now seeking to soften this profile at home. Social unrest on the Boot no longer simmers; it is boiling. And the Vatican, as the money and the power behind many of Italy's companies, does not want ever to be placed in the embarrassing position of sitting at the bargaining table opposite union leaders who are demanding more pay and more economic and social justice. Nor does the Vatican want the responsibility of firing workers or closing down plants in a shaky Italian economy. The image of Vatican capitalism now hangs like an albatross around the neck of Pope Paul.

Thus the Vatican is quietly, bit by bit, beginning to divest itself of its Italian business and industrial holdings and to invest funds outside Italy. A key man in this operation is Michele Sindona, a fifty-one-year-old Sicilian lawyer who is among the top financiers and industrialists in Italy. Having worked tirelessly over the last twenty years to win the confidence and respect of American companies, Mr. Sindona today can draw on a vast reserve of funds and goodwill from the United States. He has at his beck and call an international commission of eighteen businessmen, appointed by Pope Paul several years ago, to give him professional advice. This advisory commission includes James A. Farley, former Postmaster General of the United States; John S. Bugas, vice-president of the Ford Motor Company; Martin R. Gainsbrugh, chief economist of the U. S. National Industrial Conference Board; and Vermont C. Royster, senior vice-president and editor of *The Wall Street Journal*.

Through Mr. Sindona the Vatican has sold to Gulf & Western Industries most of its interest (retaining only about 5 percent) in Italy's largest real-estate and construction company, the $175-million Società Generale Immobiliare, the same company that built the huge Watergate apartment complex for $70 million in Washington, D.C.* (In Italy, S.G.I. is responsible for thousands of buildings and other construction projects. The company put up three quarters of the money to build the posh Cavalieri Hilton Hotel. And, for the 1960 Olympic Games, S.G.I. got the government to build on its

* See Chapter 1 for a more elaborate treatment of the subject.

land an unnecessarily circuitous highway to connect Olympic installations in the northern and southern sections of the city. It might also be added that these installations were constructed by S.G.I. and its front companies.)

By applying the economic brakes, Mr. Sindona is leading the Vatican through the tangled jungles of big business and the swirling waters of Madison Avenue image-building to stop the proverbial economic tail from wagging the hefty ecclesiastical dog. In September 1971 Mr. Sindona and a syndicate of international businessmen took over the Rome *Daily American*, Italy's only English-language daily newspaper, now in its twenty-seventh year of publication. This acquisition was deemed important enough by the Sindona strategy because it gives the Vatican an opportunity to control its first newspaper not in the Italian language.

The Vatican's American investments are largely concentrated in real estate and stockholding, and much of the business is done through the Chase Manhattan Bank, the First National City Bank and the Continental Illinois Bank. The Vatican portfolio today includes stocks in Celanese, Chase Manhattan, Colgate, Dan River, General Foods, Merck, Procter & Gamble, Standard Oil, Unilever and Westinghouse— companies that the Vatican financial experts consider solid gainers. Altogether, it can be safely stated that the Vatican owns no less than $2 billion worth of securities on the New York Stock Exchange.

A substantial part of the $3 billion being spent in the present urban transformation of lower Manhattan by the Uris Building Corporation and Tishman Realty & Construction is being provided by the Vatican, which is also involved in the building of the 300-acre World Trade Center.

Esteemed by the financial community as a wizard of odds, Mr. Sindona still has several more years of chessboard strategy before he frees the Vatican from the fetters of Italian public opinion and transfers the pontifical wealth to other parts of the world, while keeping Vatican income high. The watchdog is only just beginning to nose-nudge the Vatican's not inconsiderable problem of changing the sign of the dollar back to the sign of the cross.

Even though the Sindona policy may still be in its formative stages, we can observe the direction it is taking. Among some of Mr. Sindona's early accomplishments was the agreement made in the fall of 1969 by the Vatican, the Fiat automobile company and the Italian government for the sale of Lancia, Italy's fourth-largest car firm. The Vatican, which owned a third of Lancia's shares and which had one of its "men of trust," Massimo Spada, serving as chairman of the Lancia board, sold out its holding to Giovanni Agnelli of Fiat for a token sum of $150,000 (based on the agreed rate of one lira each—.0016 of a penny—for shares that were worth 1,000 lire apiece at the time). The Lancia transaction was effected after three weeks of negotiations among Mr. Sindona, Mr. Agnelli and officers of the Italian government, which owned a majority interest in the Lancia company. Under the terms of the deal, the Pope agreed to pay Lancia's $160.8 million debt, for which he accepted Mr. Agnelli's I.O.U. Meanwhile, the Fiat president is undertaking to put Lancia auto production back on a paying basis.

Another big Italian firm that had been bound to the Vatican and that has been given the Sindona ax treatment is Montecatini Edison. Italy's largest company and the eighth-largest outside the United States, this giant chemical group reported total sales of $930 million during 1969 and a net profit of $66.7 million. Although the extent of papal participation in Montecatini Edison was never fully known, the Vatican decided in 1969 to divorce itself from this major corporation by unloading the stock it held. Quietly the Vatican-held shares fell into the hands of I.R.I. and E.N.I., two Italian state holding companies, an action that has raised protests from stockholders all over Italy as they see what was once the nation's largest privately owned firm come under the growing influence of the Italian government.

Keeping up with Mr. Sindona's activity is a kind of game that many of the correspondents in Rome are trying their hand at. But "Sindona watching," as it's called, is a difficult game to play, because Mr. Sindona's activities are not easily observed. This is not to suggest that what Mr. Sindona does on behalf of the Vatican is either illegal or unethical; suffice it to say that it is too complicated to follow, especially since, understandably, his negotiations are carried out under the tightest security—indubitably classified as "Sacred" and "Top Sacred."

Typical of the maneuvering engaged in by the Vatican and Mr. Sindona is the following illustration. As mentioned earlier, the Vatican-controlled Italcementi Company, the largest cement company in Italy, has a heavy interest in a financial company called Italmobiliare. The latter in turn owns dozens and dozens of other companies, each of which also owns dozens and dozens of other companies—some of which own bits of each other and interests in the Italcementi Company.* Some of the stock of Italmobiliare is in the hands of such financial institutions as the Banca Provinciale Lombarda, Credito Commerciale and Bastogi, each of which is Vatican controlled. The last-named company (Bastogi) is the organization through which the Vatican, Italcementi and Mr. Sindona got rid of their stocks in the Montecatini Edison chemical conglomerate and acquired stock in the Assicurazioni Generali, the largest insurance company in Italy. The Assicurazioni Generali, in turn, has a half interest in the Molini Biondi spaghetti company, the other half being owned by the Vati-

* The reader is reminded that in Italy, unlike the United States, holding companies are not illegal.

can and the Molini Pantanella spaghetti company, which happens to be owned half by the Vatican and half by the Assicurazioni Generali. This financial institution also had a heavy financial interest in S.G.I., the construction company of which Mr. Sindona is now a director and in which the Vatican until recently had substantial holdings, which it sold to Gulf & Western.

But to get back to Bastogi, this company now owns about 10 percent of the Italcementi Company. And in recent months, Mr. Sindona has acquired under his own name more than 1.2 million shares (from the Vatican and other sellers) of the Bastogi securities. This may sound like the Rube Goldberg version of Monopoly, but, to be perfectly frank, I have deliberately left out more than half of the explanation in order to "clarify" it.

Given the talents of men like Sindona, it is no wonder that the Vatican has become what is perhaps the world's biggest conglomerate. The activities of the Vatican sometimes irk people who have to deal with it, but it has been that way for centuries. Napoleon, for example, once showed his disdain during a talk with Ercole Cardinal Consalvi, who became Secretary of State to Pope Pius VII in 1800.

"Do you understand, I am capable of destroying your Church?" sneered the exasperated Corsican.

Unmoved and unperturbed, Cardinal Consalvi snapped back with a rejoinder that has now become a classic: "Sir, not even we priests have achieved that in eighteen centuries!"

BIBLIOGRAPHY

[This is a minimal listing of references, all published during the last decade. For any reader who wants to familiarize himself with the Catholic Church and its economic and social position in the United States, many of the listed sources have useful bibliographies on the general areas covered in this book.]

ABBOTT, WALTER M., S.J. (editor), *The Documents of Vatican II*, New York, Association Press, 1966.

ARMSTRONG, O.K., "Tax Churches on Business Profits?" *Christianity Today*, October 13, 1961, pp. 19–23.

BALK, ALFRED, *The Religion Business*, Richmond, John Knox, 1968.

BLANSHARD, PAUL, *Paul Blanshard on Vatican II*, Boston, Beacon Press, 1966.

———, *Religion and the Schools: The Great Controversy*, Boston, Beacon Press, 1963.

BUEHRER, EDWIN T., *The Changing Climate of Religion*, New York, Pageant, 1965.

CALLAHAN, DANIEL (editor), *Federal Aid and Catholic Schools*, Baltimore, Helicon, 1964.

CAVALLARI, ALBERTO, *The Changing Vatican*, London, Faber & Faber, 1968.

CLAYTON, A. STAFFORD, *Religion and Schooling*, Waltham, Blaisdell, 1969.

COGDELL, GASTON D., *What Price Parochiaid?*, Washington, Americans United, 1970.

COHEN, LAWRENCE P., "Constitutionality of Tax Exemptions Accorded American Church Property," *Albany Law Review*, January 1966, pp. 58–69.

CURRY, JAMES E., *Public Regulation of the Religious Use of Land*, Charlottesville, Mitchie, 1964.

DOERR, EDD, *The Conspiracy That Failed*, Washington, Americans United, 1968.

DORIS, LILLIAN (editor), *The American Way in Taxation: Internal Revenue, 1862–1963*, New York, Prentice-Hall, 1963.

DRINAN, ROBERT F., *Religion, The Courts and Public Policy*, New York, McGraw-Hill, 1963.

DROUIN, BROTHER EDMOND G., *The School Question: A Bibliography of Church-State Relationships in American Education— 1940–1960*, Washington, Catholic University of America Press, 1963.

EISENSTEIN, LOUIS, *The Ideologies of Taxation*, New York, Ronald Press, 1961.

ELFENBEIN, HIRAM, *Organization Religion*, New York, Philosophical Library, 1968.

FELLMAN, DAVID, *Religion in American Public Law*, Boston, Boston University Press, 1965.

FREUND, PAUL, and ROBERT ULICH, *Religion and the Public Schools*, Cambridge, Harvard University Press, 1965.

FRIEDLANDER, ANNA FAY, *The Shared Time Strategy*, St. Louis, Concordia, 1966.

GANNON, ROBERT I., S.J., *The Cardinal Spellman Story*, Garden City, Doubleday, 1962.

HACKER, LOUIS M. (editor), *Major Documents in American Economic History*, Princeton, D. Van Nostrand, 1961.

HEALEY, ROBERT M., *Jefferson on Religion in Public Education*, New Haven, Yale University Press, 1962.

HELLERSTEIN, JEROME R., *Taxes, Loopholes and Morals*, New York, McGraw-Hill, 1963.

HOOK, SIDNEY, *Religion in a Free Society*, Lincoln, University of Nebraska Press, 1967.

HOWE, MARK, *The Garden and the Wilderness*, Chicago, University of Chicago Press, 1965.

HUEGLI, ALBERT G. (editor), *Church and State Under God*, St. Louis, Concordia, 1964.

HUGHES, PHILIP, *A Short History of the Catholic Church*, London, Burns & Oates, 1967.

JEANES, SAMUEL A., "Should Church Property Be Taxed?," *Church Management*, September 1962, pp. 8–11.

KATZ, WILBUR G., *Religion and the American Constitution*, Evanston, Northwestern University Press, 1964.

KAUPER, PAUL G., *Civil Liberties and the Constitution*, Ann Arbor, University of Michigan Press, 1962.

————, *Religion and the Constitution*, Baton Rouge, Louisiana State University Press, 1964.

KAVANAUGH, REV. JAMES, *A Modern Priest Looks At His Outdated Church*, New York, Trident Press/A Division of Simon & Schuster, 1967.

KERWIN, JEROME G., *Catholic Viewpoint on Church and State*, Garden City, Hanover House, 1960.

KURLAND, PHILIP B., *Of Church and State and the Supreme Court*, Chicago, University of Chicago Law School, 1961.

————, *Religion and the Law*, Chicago, Aldine, 1962.

LANNING, GEOFFREY J., "Tax Erosion and the 'Bootstrap Sale' of a Business—I," *University of Pennsylvania Law Review*, March 1960, pp. 623–696.

LA NOUE, GEORGE R., *Public Funds for Parochial Schools*, New York, National Council of Churches, 1963.

LARSON, MARTIN A., *Church Wealth and Business Income*, New York, Philosophical Library, 1965.

LARSON, MARTIN A., and C. STANLEY LOWELL, *Praise the Lord for Tax Exemption*, Washington/New York, Robert B. Luce, 1969.

233

LEE, JAMES MICHAEL, *Catholic Education in the Western World,* Notre Dame, University of Notre Dame Press, 1967.

LITTELL, FRANKLIN HAMLIN, *From State Church to Pluralism,* Garden City, Doubleday, 1962.

LO BELLO, NINO, *The Vatican Empire,* New York, Trident Press/ A Division of Simon & Schuster, 1968.

LODER, JAMES E., *Religion and the Public Schools,* New York, Association Press, 1965.

LOWELL, C. STANLEY, *Embattled Wall,* Washington, Americans United, 1966.

———, *Federal Aid to Parochial Schools* (Congressional Testimony), Washington, Americans United, 1961.

LUNDBERG, FERDINAND, *The Rich and the Super-Rich,* New York, Lyle Stuart, 1968.

MANHATTAN, AVRO, *Catholic Power Today,* New York, Lyle Stuart, 1967.

MANWARING, DAVID R., *Render Unto Caesar,* Chicago, University of Chicago Press, 1962.

MARNELL, WILLIAM H., *The First Amendment: The History of Religious Freedom in America,* New York, Doubleday, 1964.

MARTY, MARTIN, JOSEPH MOODY and ATHUR HERZBERG, *The Outbursts That Await Us,* New York, Macmillan, 1963.

MCGRATH, JOHN J., *Church and State in American Law,* Milwaukee, Bruce, 1962.

MCGURN, BARRETT, *A Reporter Looks at American Catholicism,* New York, Hawthorn, 1967.

———, *A Reporter Looks at the Vatican,* New York, Coward-McCann, 1962.

MCLOUGHLIN, EMMETT, *American Culture and Catholic Schools,* New York, Lyle Stuart, 1960.

MENDELSOHN, JACK, "Moral Concerns and Economic Strength: The Investment Philosophy of Organized Religion," *Worldview,* April 1967, pp. 6–8.

MORGAN, RICHARD E., *The Politics of Religious Conflict,* New York, Pegasus, 1968.

NATIONAL CATHOLIC WELFARE CONFERENCE, "The Constitutionality of the Inclusion of Church-Related Schools in Federal Aid to Education," Washington, N.C.W.C. Legal Department, 1961.

NEUWIEN, REGINALD A., *Catholic Schools in Action*, Notre Dame, University of Notre Dame Press, 1966.

NEVILLE, ROBERT, *The World of the Vatican*, New York, Harper & Row, 1962.

OAKS, DOLLIN H., *The Wall Between Church and State*, Baton Rouge, Louisiana State University Press, 1963.

O'CONNOR, JOHN, *The People Versus Rome*, New York, Random House, 1969.

O'HAIR, MADALYN MURRAY, *What on Earth Is an Atheist?*, Austin, American Atheist Press, 1969.

PALLENBERG, CORRADO, *Le Finanze del Vaticano*, Milan, Palazzi Editore, 1969.

PEARSON, DREW, and JACK ANDERSON, *The Case Against Congress*, New York, Simon and Schuster, 1968.

PECHMAN, JOSEPH A., *Federal Tax Policy*, Washington, The Brookings Institution, 1966.

PFEFFER, LEO, *Church, State and Freedom* (revised edition), Boston, Beacon Press, 1966.

PRATT, JOHN WEBB, *Religion, Politics and Diversity: The Church-State Theme in New York History*, Ithaca, Cornell University Press, 1967.

RAAB, EARL (editor), *Religious Conflict in America*, Garden City, Doubleday, 1964.

ROBERTSON, D. B., *Should Churches Be Taxed?*, Philadelphia, Westminster, 1968.

RYAN, MARY PERKINS, *Are Parochial Schools the Answer?*, New York, Holt, Rinehart & Winston, 1964.

RYAN, REV. JOHN A., and FRANCIS J. BOLAND, *Catholic Principles of Politics: The State and the Church*, New York, Macmillan, 1960.

SALISBURY, W. SEWARD, *Religion in American Culture: A Sociological Interpretation*, Homewood, Dorsey Press, 1964.

SANDERS, THOMAS G., *Protestant Concepts of Church and State*, New York, Holt, Rinehart & Winston, 1964.

SENG, MICHAEL, "Federal Taxation—Capital Gains Treatment Given Proceeds from Bootstrap Transfer of Corporation to Tax-Exempt Organization," *Notre Dame Lawyer*, December 1965, pp. 273–278.

SHUSTER, GEORGE N., *Catholic Education in a Changing World*, New York, Holt, Rinehart & Winston, 1967.

SMITH, ELWYN A., *Church and State in Your Community*, Philadelphia, Westminster, 1963.

Special to the N.C.R.: The First Five Years of the National Catholic Reporter, Kansas City, *National Catholic Reporter*, 1969.

STERN, PHILIP M., *The Great Treasury Raid*, New York, New American Library, 1965.

STOKES, ANSON PHELPS, and LEO PFEFFER, *Church and State in the United States*, New York, Harper & Row, 1964.

STROUP, HERBERT, *Church and State in Confrontation*, New York, Seabury, 1967.

SWOMLEY, JOHN M., Jr., *Religion, the State and the Schools*, New York, Pegasus, 1968.

"Taxing the Churches: The Law and the Facts," *America*, June 3, 1967, p. 801.

TUSSMAN, JOSEPH, *The Supreme Court on Church and State*, New York, Oxford Press, 1962.

VELVEL, LAWRENCE R., "Taxation—Federal Income Taxation: The Three-Party Sale and Lease-Back," *Michigan Law Review*, April 1963, pp. 1140–1158.

WARD, LEO, C.S.C., *Federal Aid to Private Schools*, Westminster, Newman Press, 1964.

WEBER, MAX, *General Economic History*, New York, Collier Books, 1961.

WECHSBERG, JOSEPH, *The Merchant Bankers*, New York, Little, Brown, 1966.

WHELAN, C. M., "Tax Exemption," *New Catholic Encyclopedia*, New York, McGraw-Hill, 1967.

"Will Churches Pay Taxes?" *Christianity Today*, July 8, 1966, p. 42.

WILLIAMS, WILLIAM A., *The Contours of American History,* New York, World, 1966.

ZIEGLER, EDWARD, *The Vested Interests,* New York, Macmillan, 1964.